TENACITY

Tenacity

PENCILING THE JOURNEY AND INKING THE DESTINY

VEENA SHARMA

LUMINARE PRESS
WWW.LUMINAREPRESS.COM

Printed in the United States of America

Cover Design by Melissa K. Thomas

Luminare Press
442 Charnelton St.
Eugene, OR 97401
www.luminarepress.com

LCCN: 2020909285
ISBN: 978-1-64388-386-1

Dedication

In memory of my dad.
Thank you for your love and guidance to become who
I am today. Hope you are proud of your little princess.

To my loving mom,
who helped me to become the woman I am today.

To my children, who always supported me.
You are the greatest blessing in my life.

To everyone who influenced and inspired me to become
who I am today.

To everyone who helped me with this book.

*Destiny is not a matter of chance;
it is a matter of choice. It is not a thing to be
waited for, it is a thing to be achieved.*

—William Jennings Bryan

Table of Contents

Introduction 1

CHAPTER ONE
Appreciate Simple Things in Life 5

CHAPTER TWO
Change Helps Us Grow 22

CHAPTER THREE
Never Take Anything for Granted 31

CHAPTER FOUR
Buried Under Cultural Burden 46

CHAPTER FIVE
Live Life with Purpose and Intent 69

CHAPTER SIX
Be a Visionary Person 89

CHAPTER SEVEN
Moving Forward in Life 100

CHAPTER EIGHT
Recreating My Footprints 119

CONCLUSION
Follow Your Dreams 135

Introduction

During our journey of life, we come across many obstacles and barriers which prevent us from achieving our goals or prevent us from becoming the person we want to become. The choice is ours; either we let those barriers and obstacles control us, or we take control of our life, and create the life we desire.

Be miserable. Or motivate yourself. Whatever has to be done, it's always your choice.

—DR. WAYNE DYER

My story begins on April 28, 1964, in a place called the Fiji Islands. Fiji is located in Melanesia, in the South Pacific, consisting of more than three hundred islands. People say those who visit or live there think it is pure paradise. Having been to many of the Caribbean Islands, although very beautiful in their own right, I can say that they don't compare to Fiji. One could easily say that nothing compares to your home growing up. Indeed, I would agree. The serenity, which includes the beauty, diverse culture, and sense of belonging in Fiji, is unparalleled. Geographically, Fiji contains two major islands: Viti Levu and Vanua Levu. I'm from Viti Levu, a gorgeous island that happens to be the location of the main international airport. Fiji is known for its rugged landscape, sandy beaches, palm trees, coral lagoons, colorful soft corals, tropical flowers, and fruits.

Additionally, there are kava and fire walking ceremonies, inviting family activities, cultural diversity, and friendly, easy-going, island-time oriented people. Fiji's population consists of two principal ethnic groups: Melanesian-Polynesian, referred to as Fijians, and Indians who migrated to Fiji, called Indo-Fijians. My grandparents from my father's side and my great grandparents from my mother's side came from India. Therefore, I am an Indo-Fijian, born in Fiji, with Indian heritage.

Let me shed a little light on the settlement of Indians in Fiji. Between the years 1879 and 1916, a total of 60,000 Indians were brought to Fiji as indentured laborers to work on sugarcane plantations. British agents recruited Indians with the promise of high pay and a better lifestyle. The majority of the recruited Indians were poor and uneducated. Socioeconomically speaking, they were easy targets. Girmit was an agreement between the British Government and the Indian laborers. The Indian indentured laborer's workday was long, starting as early as three o'clock in the morning and ending late in the evening. Work conditions were very harsh and demanding. The Girmit agreement was for a term of five years but was renewable for another five years.

Approximately twenty-five thousand of the original sixty thousand returned to India, and the rest of them made Fiji their home. My grandparents decided to stay in Fiji and bought hundreds of acres of land in a very remote area of Fiji called Dawasamu. It was all beachfront farmland. Before passing away, my grandfather distributed the property among his sons—my father and uncles. That is where I was born and spent the majority of my childhood. My mom and dad had an arranged marriage, and she was only fifteen when they married. There are seven siblings in the family, five brothers and two sisters. My sister is the oldest and I am the youngest. One of my brothers passed away about fifteen years ago of a heart condition. Though my parents got an education in Catholic schools, like my grandfather, my father took over the farm and became a farmer, and my mom stayed home to look after us children.

Reflecting back on my life, it was a journey filled with both good and bad experiences, obstacles and opportunities. Everything has a purpose in life; at least that's what I believe. Excellent skills empower and motivate us, whereas challenging, or what some would call negative experiences, teach us something. We need both to shape the person we become. When we accept the challenge, we turn it into strength.

As people say, "When life gives you lemons, make lemonade."

Today, I am thankful to everyone in my life who had an influence, whether positive or negative, because I would not be who I am today were they not in my life. Every experience has taken me one step closer to where I want to be. Nothing comes easily in life, but anything is possible if you believe in yourself.

―――――― GOLDEN NUGGET ――――――

From my perspective, every experience and every person we meet serves a purpose in our life, either good or bad. Your experience in life, including mistakes, struggles, and failures, doesn't have to define who you are, but instead, it can indeed lead you to discover your true self.

CHAPTER ONE

Appreciate Simple Things in Life

Pause to appreciate the beauty around you.
Whether rainbow or butterfly,
mountain or tree, painting or poem -
whether crafted by nature or by a human hand -
beauty adds a magical element to life
that surpasses logic and science.

—JONATHAN LOCKWOOD HUIE

I t was an evening in Fort Myers, Florida, where I live now. I was preparing to leave and visit the place where I was born and had lived until age sixteen. The location is called Fiji. Fiji is an island in the South Pacific, approximately a seventeen-hour plane ride from Fort Myers, Florida. It was exhilarating and sad at the same time, sort of bittersweet. The task at hand was to rush home from work and get my packing done. Hours of preparation packing and organizing the house, all at the same time, left me feeling exhausted. It was hard for me to fall asleep that night as memories began racing through my mind. It was easy to picture myself when I was a little girl, which made it difficult to fall asleep. I heard my mom sing, "You are my sunshine, my only sunshine. You make me happy when skies are gray," as if she was right in front of me.

Mom used to sing me to sleep as a little girl, and just the thought of her singing to me worked to put me to sleep. Speaking of present-day reality and not my dreams, everything is so different now. My dad passed away a few years ago, and my mom is aging, unable to do things she used to. Making matters more challenging, she lives in Vancouver, Canada, in an extended care facility, and I live in Florida.

With my mom when I was 2 years old.
Taken at my uncle's photo studio, Suva, Fiji Islands.

Veena Sharma

When I finally woke up the next morning, it was already time to leave for the airport. The Southwest International Airport is about a twenty-minute drive from my house. Quickly, I grabbed some coffee and breakfast on the way to the airport. It was so exciting that there was no hesitation, and mostly I was ready for the long flight back to the place where I grew up and had made many beautiful memories. Sitting in the window seat and looking outside, I was thinking about my life as a little girl growing up in the beautiful Fiji Islands. This paradise of my childhood is a place deep in my soul, and I have never been able to let go, even though it has been almost forty years since I left. Experiences came back as if it were just yesterday. It was as if there was a movie projector playing in the back of my mind, allowing me to picture everything. When I was a little girl, boat, bus, and car were the only modes of transportation, unlike what is available now. In Dawasamu, my dad crafted, by hand, a twenty-foot wooden boat with three wooden benches and a forty horsepower Johnson outboard motor. Surrounding communities depended on my dad and his boat for transportation and fishing. It had seating for six, but he usually carried many more people out of pure necessity. Two indigenous Fijian villages existed on each side of our home, two miles away.

Our six-bedroom, one-level wooden house with a tin peaked roof was built on a hill, about a mile from the beach. The kitchen had an old cast iron English wood burning cooking stove. My grandfather designed the house and built it with help from friends, family, and villagers. The materials used were from a bed and breakfast guest house on the island of Levuka, about ten miles across the ocean. My dad ran underground piping from a small stream approximately a mile from the house, so we had fresh Fiji spring water in our home. He had placed water filters in the pipe to prevent debris, fish, shrimp, frogs, etc. from getting into the pipeline.

My childhood home in Dawasamu, Fiji Islands.

We had horses, chickens, and cows. My brothers were assigned to milk the cows every morning, so we had fresh milk. Our yard was full of fresh fruit, including mangoes, bananas, guavas, mandarin, breadfruit, soursop, watermelon, passion fruit, lemons, limes, ugly fruit, star fruit, and cantaloupe. We grew up eating organic fruits, vegetables, and meat. Everything we ate was freshly harvested and consumed right away as we did not have electricity to run a refrigerator. Life was simple and stress-free. For me, unlike most of the other kids my age, childhood was not about attending school. Instead, it was all about adventure. Everything I saw and encountered fascinated me. Birds flying made me think about how lucky they were to go so easily and freely to places otherwise unseen.

Tropical flowers, including hibiscus, plumeria, jasmine, and gardenia, were my favorites. My mom planted a tropical flower garden by the porch at the front of the house. My first love of tropical flowers permeated my entire soul, and indeed they are now part of my tropical garden in Florida. You might take the girl out of Fiji, but you can never take Fiji out of the girl. It was captivating to me to see how the caterpillars turned into beautiful butterflies. At the time, although I did not understand metamorphosis and did not question it, I thoroughly appreciated it. Everything around me made me think about how beautiful was my part of the world.

Every morning after eating breakfast freshly made by my mom, I ran downhill, barefoot, from my house, wearing a dress made by my mom. I could feel the sand under my little feet and the ocean breeze brushing my long, uncombed, dark hair while I ran downhill about a mile to the beach. On the way, I saw my dad and my brothers, Nesh, Bob, and Ravi working on the farm. Not wanting anyone to stop me, I ran right by them as fast as I could. One day, I got a well-deserved spanking. The adventure was my mission to accomplish, not to work in the farm. Some said I was a little princess. That worked for me! Every morning, I longed to get to the beach before the tide started coming in. I walked on the wet sand to the reef to see the beauty of the underwater world exposed for precious little time. Blue, red, and orange corals were set against the deep blue sea in the background, with the colorful fish coming up to say hello as the waves bounced against the edge of the reef. Mesmerized, I stood on the side of the beach, looking at the deep blue sea until I heard someone calling me, usually my dad or brother, Nesh. The experience of looking into the deep sea was like imagery meditation, which I was unaware of at that time. The underwater world always amazed me for some reason, but the danger of standing there alone, especially when I did not know how to swim, never really crossed my mind. What if I fell in the water? Would anyone find me? Fearlessly, I stood at the edge of the reef, admiring the beauty of the ocean. Before going back home, I collected some seashells, especially cowrie shells, to add to my shell collection.

Excited about my new collection, I ran back home, shouting with excitement, "Mom, Dad, look, I got so many shells."

My dad replied, "Vinnu, what are you going to do with all the shells? You already have enough."

By then, lunch was ready. My mom dug from the farm and boiled fresh cassava root, which is much like a potato. She prepared spinach and vegetables cooked in freshly squeezed coconut milk, pressed by hand. My mom grated the white flesh of the coconut, added hot water, and squeezed the coconut to get the coconut milk. It was amazing to watch my mom cook. I sometimes helped her because I wanted to learn how to cook. There was no canned coconut milk as there is nowadays. Everything my mom made was from scratch. Maybe this is when my love for cooking developed. Even though times have changed and there are items available to make life easier, like my mom, I still choose to cook some stuff from scratch. There is some kind of personal satisfaction involved, and also it takes me back to those good old days.

After eating lunch, I took the shells to my secret play area under the porch, which I had created. I did not know what it was like to have friends to play with or to have toys. Through my imagination, I created a play area. My creative play area was a leveled sand floor, little houses built with rocks and twigs, with cowrie shells representing people. Everything in my play area represented something. It was a world of my own making.

Our property had many things to keep everyone occupied. At the back of our house, about a mile away, was a stream that led to the ocean. After lunch, I headed down to the stream with my brother, Munna, who is a few years older than me. One area of the flow was full and had lots of large trees. Munna and I had a dinghy hidden there, which we found on the beach after a tropical storm. We occasionally took the dinghy out in the ocean to catch fish without our parents' knowledge. We took the dinghy out when the tide was high, so we were able to row out to the ocean and back using the stream. We then tied it to a mangrove tree root. We kept the dinghy until its owner from the neighboring village claimed it. My brother Munna did get a lecture from my dad about the danger we exposed ourselves to, plus keeping something that didn't belong to us. My dad was a man of principle. Neither my DNA nor my brain contained a fear of deep water or other creatures existing in the water, so adventure was the only thing on my mind.

December was a unique month for me in Fiji. It was time to go to the city with my family to my grandparents' house to celebrate Christmas. It was time to see my grandparents, uncles, aunts, and cousins. Carefully, I packed some clothes in my little old bag, which I received as a gift from a relative. Early the morning of departure, I ran outside to have a shower in the stand-alone building that had a bathroom with a shower built by my dad. All I was thinking about was how much fun I would have with my cousins. Purposefully, I wore my best dress for the trip to Suva City. I did not have fancy or expensive dresses, clothing, or shoes, as did my well-to-do cousins. There was no intended competition with them, but I did want to impress them and be able to fit in. After I got ready, I went in front of my mom and dad and danced with joy, showing off myself. My mom and dad hugged me and told me how beautiful I looked, even though I had a few teeth missing and a crooked smile due to that. Thinking about what was next, I could not get my mind off the fun time that was waiting for me. Even though I realized we had a long journey to the grandparents' house, it did nothing to reduce my anticipation or excitement. The only way to get to the city was to ride my dad's little wooden boat to catch the bus.

With Dad, Mom, Munna, and I working together, we were able to get on the boat despite heavy rocking in the wind and waves while boarding. My dad skillfully navigated the boat toward the river's edge, where the bus was waiting for us. Along the way, we passed a few villages and waved to everyone with excitement. Everyone on the shore would get excited and run to the water's edge, knowing we were city bound. Some of those villagers had never been to the city. Finally, we arrived at the bus station and boarded the bus. It was a long bus ride to the town where my grandparents were waiting for us. It was natural to fall asleep on the way, but I woke up when the bus stopped. After seeing grandma waving at us, I jumped from my seat and wiggled my little body out of the bus without waiting for my parents. Quickly, I ran to my grandma, who was impatiently waiting for me with a bag of candies. Tears started rolling from my eyes when my grandma hugged me. I didn't want to let go of my grandma's hand. I stood there, holding my grandma's hand tightly until the taxi arrived to take us home. Additionally, I was looking forward to seeing my cousins, who were my age.

The taxi finally arrived at my grandparents' house, which looked like a mansion in comparison to our place. Being shy, I quickly got behind my parents, embarrassed, as my cousins and the rest of the family came out to greet us. From the corner of my eye, I saw my cousins and the dresses and shoes they were wearing. Then I looked at my old home-sewn dress and worn flip-flops. My parents' income was crop-dependent, and it was all they could afford. My grandparents owned a family business in the city. My uncles were very wealthy, so my cousins had the best outfits. Deep down, I wished I could have all of that, but at that time thought it was not possible. Sometimes my cousins gave me their old dresses that they didn't want anymore, and I was hoping that I would get a few dresses from this time also. That evening, my grandparents, as usual, had arranged for a family dinner at home. It was one of my favorite times as everyone got to eat together. Per tradition, I sat at the table next to my beloved cousin Dev. At home, we did not use utensils such as forks, spoons, or knives. It was the old-fashioned country kind of living, using your hands to eat. My cousin Dev showed me how to hold the utensils. Carefully, I followed her as I did not want to embarrass anyone.

The evening ended with the family watching a Charlie Chaplin movie in my grandparents' movie room. The movie room was in the middle of the house, with a projector and screen. We all sat on the floor while my uncle operated the projector. That night, I slept in Dev's room. The room was beautifully decorated with a white double bed and a white dresser with a mirror. The windows had pink curtains. The bed was very comfortable. I wished one day I could have a room of my own just like that. Dev told me stories about her school and the friends she had. She said that they played on a swing, and her friends came to her house to play dress up. Nothing she said made sense to me as all I knew was the play area I had created under the porch of my house. Dev fell asleep before I did. All I kept thinking about was everything Dev had told me, and I wished I could be in school and have friends to play with, too. Reality greeted me as I realized that it was not possible as there weren't any schools where I lived. Shortly, I fell asleep thinking about school, friends, Christmas, presents, and meeting Santa.

The next morning, like every Christmas, my grandma had planned to take all of us to meet Santa and get family pictures. That morning, I was sad due to not having a new dress to wear for the picture. It was tradition for all the cousins to get a picture taken at my uncle's photo studio before going to Santa. To my surprise, Dev let me borrow one of her dresses to wear for the picture and to visit Santa. It was a pink ballerina style dress with lots of ruffles. I wore it carefully to make sure it did not get ripped or torn in any way. After putting it on, I looked at myself in the mirror and couldn't believe my eyes as to how pretty I looked in that dress. The dress was exceptional and looked good on me. I wanted that dress so badly, and it was easy to become very sad knowing that it was a costly dress, and I would never be able to have it. The department store was within short walking distance, and I walked excitedly, holding my grandma's hand tightly, so I wouldn't get lost in the crowd. Christmas decorations were on display throughout the city, with a huge Christmas tree and lots of toys in the store. Santa was wearing a red and white outfit with matching hat and had a long, white beard. He was sitting in a beautiful and large sofa style red velvet chair with a line of little kids waiting for their chance to sit on his lap. Excitement got my heart beating faster the closer I got to Santa. Finally, it was my turn, and I went and sat quietly on Santa's lap. Santa told me how pretty I looked and gave me a present. It was a big box, more significant than any other gifts I'd received before.

Anxious about the contents, I quickly opened the box and couldn't believe my eyes. It was a doll, my first. The doll came with a blue outfit, and with help from my dad, I named it Kennedy. Occasionally, I have wondered why we called that doll Kennedy. I even asked my brothers, but they didn't know either, which means the reason we named the doll Kennedy will forever remain a mystery. It was the best Christmas ever, due to the fact that I received a doll, which I'd never had before. I had always wanted a doll, but my parents couldn't afford to buy one. Christmas has always been my favorite holiday, and I have kept the tradition of getting family together and exchanging presents. Even when there were times I struggled financially, I still kept the tradition as I always remember the excitement of family time and receiving gifts as a kid. Great Christmas memories from my childhood will be treasured forever. To this day, I continue the Christmas tradition of family get-togethers and gift exchanges.

The best and most beautiful things in the world cannot be seen or even touched. They must be felt with the heart.

—HELEN KELLER

After spending two wonderful weeks with my grandparents and cousins, it was time for us to go back home. It was a sad day for me as, during the previous couple of weeks, I had my cousins to play and watch movies with. A strong realization overcame me, knowing I would miss them when playing alone in my secret play area at home by myself. Finally, I went to say goodbye to Dev, and to my surprise, Dev hugged me and told me that I could have the dress. Very distinctly, I remember running to my mom and asking, "Mom, Dev gave me this dress, can I please keep it?"

My mom was quiet for a while and went to talk to Dev's mom. My anxiety increased when thinking, *what if my mom says no?* After what seemed like forever, although probably just a brief moment, my mom came to me and said that I could keep the dress. My heart filled with joy, and I went to Dev and gave her a big hug goodbye. With additional reservations about not wanting a great time to end, I also said my goodbyes to everyone else and started heading home with my family. It was a long ride back home on the bus. It rained heavily. The bus stopped at the river's edge for us to get on the boat. Unfortunately, due to the heavy rain, the river flooded. Flooding after heavy rain is a typical occurrence in the Fiji Islands. We stood at the edge of the river in the rain for hours until a few villagers came with a raft made from bamboo, which was the only way to cross the river. I got on the raft with the family without any fear. Once across the river, we had to walk the last few miles while crossing a swamp and experiencing several fall-downs before reaching home. It was late at night before we arrived home. The moment remains fresh in my mind, standing in front of my mom, shivering and crying. My mom dried me off, changed me into my pajamas, and kissed me goodnight. Immediately, I fell asleep in my bed, that night holding my doll, Kennedy, while my mom sang, "You are my sunshine, my only sunshine. You make me happy when skies are gray. You'll never know dear, how much I love you. Please don't take my sunshine away…"

I have continued the tradition and sing the same sweet tune to help my kids fall asleep. "You are my sunshine shine, my only sunshine," is a phrase that has special meaning for us. I have several items in my house inscribed with that saying.

April was a particularly important month of the year for me. My dad always celebrated my birthday, since I was the youngest and my dad's little princess. Like every April, my dad went to the city for a few weeks to sell crops from the farm. It was easy to miss my dad when he went away. It was raining, and I sorely missed my dad more than ever, as he would carry me around on his shoulders when it rained so my feet wouldn't get dirty. I distinctly remember a time when it was raining heavily and my brothers were planting rice. Since being outdoors was second nature to me, despite my dad telling me to stay indoors to help my mom, I insisted that I go to the farm. Worried that I may get wet and catch a cold, my dad made a little tent with an old tarp and wood for me to sit under while he and my brothers worked on the rice farm.

There was no way of communicating with my dad when he was returning to our farm. Unlike nowadays, there were no cellular phones or landlines. He typically used a conch shell horn to alert us when he was close to home. One day, I was walking on the beach with my dog named Foxy. We called her Foxy because of how she looked. She had a long, sharp face, big teeth, and a gray, tan, and white coat. While looking around to see what Foxy was barking at, all of a sudden, I realized it was my dad. Foxy recognized my dad and his boat before he even used his conch shell horn.

Excitedly, I jumped with joy and ran to the house to alert my mom and my brothers that dad's boat had finally arrived. We all went and greeted my dad and helped him unload the things he brought from the city. That night, as we all sat at the dinner table as always, I started to eat dinner before anyone else. The unique tradition of me eating first may sound crazy, but my dad had made this a standing house rule. That evening, my mom made my dad's favorite dishes: curried potatoes, roti, rice, and fish. After dinner, my dad opened his old-fashioned suitcase and took out things he brought for all of us, while I was sitting on his lap. I was looking for what he brought for me. My dad brought all of us something, but there was something in particular my dad brought for me. He and my mom seemed to be hiding something from me. It was a birthday cake and a small mouth organ that was supposed to be a surprise birthday gift. That evening, after the birthday celebration, my dad taught us how to play the mouth organ. It was a fun evening. I was always treated special by my parents and my siblings.

My thought was that it was because I was the baby, but that was not the reason.

Later in life, my parents revealed to me that I was their lucky child. Before I was born, my parents struggled financially. Things started to get better for them after I was born. According to my parents, a Hindu priest created a chart when I was born, based on Vedic astrology and numerology reading. Vedic astrology is a system that originated in ancient India, which is thought to determine the destiny of the child. The priest creates a chart based on the time, place, and movement of the zodiac sign at the time of the birth. The chart reflects your life, personality, and events in your life. A special name is given to the child based on the chart. The priest named me Kamala, meaning Lotus flower. It is also another name for the Hindu Goddess Laxmi, who is believed to bring wealth and prosperity.

> *Kamala is Sanskrit for lotus. Throughout the time the lotus flower has been a powerful spiritual symbol. A lotus has its roots in mud, at the bottom of streams and ponds. But it grows to become the most beautiful flower despite its origins. It symbolizes how we too can overcome all the obstacles on our journey toward enlightenment and flourish. It also represents growth and spiritual journey.*
>
> —MALA KAMALA

My parents wanted to keep that name sacred, so they registered me by the name, "Veena." My siblings and parents also called me by my nickname, "Vinnu." The priest told my parents that I was their lucky child and would bring them wealth and prosperity, but that the wealth would go with me when they gave me away in marriage.

As crazy it may sound, according to my family, things did get better for them after I was born. My dad occasionally talked about one particular situation which stood out. My grandfather, who had a stroke and was bedridden for a long time, passed away shortly after I was born, leaving my dad a huge death duty—a form of tax paid to the government upon inheritance of a property from a deceased person. My dad did not have any means to pay the death duty and was on the verge of losing his property. Knowing how desperate my dad was, one of his close friends from the city told him that there was someone who was interested in purchasing our property. This was all before he actually sold his property. My dad agreed, as it was better to sell the property than to lose it. The stipulation in the sale agreement was that the deposit would not be refunded if the buyers change their minds. A few weeks before the closing date, the buyers changed their minds and decided not to purchase the property. Since the deposit was nonrefundable, my dad was able to pay what he owed the government and not lose his property. Life continued on in our little paradise.

One day, while Munna and I were playing on the beach, making paper boats to release in the ocean, we saw two Caucasian people getting off a ship and looking for my dad. My older brother, Nesh, took them to my dad, and I saw my dad greet them and show them around our property. At that time, not many Caucasians visited Dawasamu, as it was a very remote and isolated place in Fiji. We were all curious as to what the deal was. That evening, while we sat at the dinner table, my dad announced that those Caucasians were from Australia and were interested in buying our property.

He also said that he would sell our property if the price was right. It was time to think about moving to the city where Munna and I would be able to attend school. My dad was a very organized man. He went over the move plan with each of us in detail. There was a chance we'd have to live in a rental house until the property in the country was sold and we could purchase a home in the city. Reflecting back on it, my dad was not only a true leader but a great mentor. He taught me many things in life, which helped me become who I am today.

GOLDEN NUGGET

No amount of worldly possessions can replace family time together. Spending time with family not only solidifies the bond between each other, but it also teaches us togetherness, caring, socialization, and values.

CHAPTER TWO

Change Helps Us Grow

Life is a series of natural and
spontaneous changes.
Don't resist them; that only creates sorrow.
Let reality be reality.
Let things flow naturally forward in
whatever way they like.

—LAO TZU

Late that year, we moved to the city. The property in the country was still under negotiation between my dad and the buyer. With the little money we had and with help from my grandparents, we started a new life in the city. My dad rented a small, three-bedroom flat for all nine of us, which meant that I had to share a room. Luckily, my parents' room was big enough to fit my twin bed in a corner. Munna and I enrolled in elementary school for the first time. After listening to Dev's story about her school life, I was looking forward to going to school and doing the same things that Dev did in her school. The day arrived for

Munna and I to go to school. Munna seemed very content, but I felt sick to my stomach just thinking about school, being away from my mom and dad, and being around strangers. My mom started braiding my long, black hair into two ponytails. I burst out crying while she was braiding my hair. All of a sudden, I started experiencing unknown fear. How would I communicate with other students? What if they did not accept me? At age nine, I still did not know how to read and write correctly. My dad, who supposedly had a good education from a Catholic school, had been teaching me reading and writing at home. My anxiety increased as thoughts of school crept through my mind. Suddenly, my heartbeat got faster and faster. I could hear my heart pounding, and I felt sweat running down my pink and white uniform. I knew that in a few minutes, I would have to leave for school and spend all day with people I did not know, and then I heard my dad's voice calling me and saying, "Vinnu, get your schoolbag. It's time to go."

I burst into tears and ran behind my mom in the kitchen. I grabbed her dress tightly and refused to let go. My mom did not say anything, just looked at my dad with an expression of feeling sorry for me. My brothers started laughing at me and called me names; chicken, weak, etc. For the first time, I saw anger in my dad's eyes. I don't know if my brothers were laughing at me, and my behavior got him irritated. All of a sudden, he grabbed my little arm and dragged me into the car while I kept screaming and resisting. There was no other choice but to get in the car. My tears had no impact on my dad. I cried riding to school, looking outside the car window, and missing my old home and my life there. I missed seeing my mom cooking, and I missed playing on the beach, walking on the edge of the reef, and enjoying the wonders of the ocean. Now, all it was just an imagination. The car finally arrived at school, and my dad grabbed my arm and took me to the principal's office, apologizing for my behavior. The principal was an older, short Indo-Fijian lady, with gray hair called Deviji. She welcomed my dad with a big smile and assured him that I would be well taken care of and told my dad that he could leave. I watched my dad walk back to the car and kept looking at him as he was walking away, while standing beside Deviji. I was hoping that he would feel sorry for his little princess and take me back home. Sometimes in life, we have to get out of our comfort zones and be taught what we call *tough love*. My dad wanted the best in life for his children, and that is the reason he sacrificed our country home and chose to move to the city. It became easier to understand this when I became a parent. He was not just my father but a great role model for me.

Tough love may be tough to give, but it is a necessity of life and assurance of positive growth.

—T. F. HODGE

The principal, Deviji, took me to my classroom and introduced me to my teacher, Ms. Seema. She was a middle-aged Indo-Fijian woman, with long, dark hair done up in a bun, and very well dressed. She came to the door as soon as she saw Deviji and took me to my desk. It was a small desk with an attached chair and a place inside for books. She welcomed me and introduced me to the class. All the kids were looking at me, and I saw some whispering to each other. I didn't know if they were talking about me, but it increased my curiosity and made me more fearful. I took my book and pencil out from the small bag my mom had bought me. After I settled, I started practicing writing as instructed by my teacher, using as well what my dad had taught me at home so far.

There was a girl named Satya who sat beside me. Satya was the same height as me but a little darker in complexion. She had long, dark hair braided in two pony tails with pink ribbon at the end of the braids. She was super helpful to me and very welcoming. After a few hours, I heard the bell ring, and everyone ran outside to play with their friends. It was recess time—our morning break. I remembered Dev talking about that. Since I did not know anyone and I was an introvert and very shy, I found a little corner outside the school building, near my classroom, and stood there, eating snacks my mom had given me. The bell rang again, and I followed everyone back in the school. Lunchtime was a little better as Satya noticed that I did not have anyone to play with or talk to, and she invited me to join her. Satya took me to the play area where we played on the swing and ropes, and jumped around, etc. It was exactly what Dev had described about her school fun time. Now everything she had told me made sense. I laughed with Satya with joy and felt much better about school by the end of the day.

The class dismissed, and it was time for everyone to go home. My dad picked me up and took me home. I did not say anything as I felt hurt and was still angry at my dad for what happened in the morning. My dad hugged me later and explained to me the importance of education, and that it was the reason for the move, anyway. I opened my bag that evening to show my mom and dad the things I did in school and realized that I had accidentally picked up Satya's pencil and brought it home with me. I felt guilty and sad because I remembered my dad telling me not to ever take anything from anyone without asking or without their permission because it is considered stealing. Many thoughts went through my mind. I didn't want Satya to think that I stole her pencil. I did not want to lose Satya's friendship. I clearly remember my dad telling me many times, "Everyone likes to take, but be the one who likes to give. There is more satisfaction in giving than receiving."

Those words from my dad inspired me, and up until now, I have learned to be a giving person. Maybe that is one of the reasons I chose a nursing career, which involves giving without expectations.

Be like the fountain that overflows, not like the cistern that merely contains.

—Paulo Coelho

I had a restless night thinking about what Satya must be thinking of me. What if she thinks that I stole the pencil from her? She was my only friend, and what if she decides not to be my friend anymore? I ran to Satya first thing the next morning, explained what happened, and returned the pencil to Satya. To my surprise, Satya didn't even realize that she was missing her pencil, but I sure felt better giving it back. We became best friends after that and spent time together in school. I have learned from my dad to always do the right thing in life even when no one is watching; it's called integrity. It is not to impress anyone but for your own good. The worst thing in life is to live with regrets. Sometimes, you never get a second chance to fix things. So, in life, I try my best not to do anything that I may regret later in life.

The time spent with Satya was precious. I often wondered what it would have been like in school if Satya wasn't there. It was time to transition from elementary school to junior high, which meant I had to change schools. By now, my attitude toward school had changed. I began to enjoy going to school. During the break before starting junior high, our property in the country was sold, which meant that we might have to move again. It was bittersweet for me. I was excited that now I would be able to live in a bigger house and have my own room, but on the flip side, I could lose Satya as a friend and might never see her again. I learned a lot from Satya. She accepted me as a friend when no one else did. She taught me to appreciate and accept people for who they are.

Many people will walk in and out of your life, but only true friends will leave footprints in your heart.

—ELEANOR ROOSEVELT

We moved into a bigger and more beautiful house with my family before the next school year started. Fortunately, the new home had everything I wanted: a big yard, my own room, a refrigerator, and a telephone. Life was getting much better and more interesting as I was growing up and getting used to the city life. I even met a few girls of the same age in the neighborhood and we became friends. I still often thought about Satya, as she had taught me about friendship and helped me build my confidence around people. Unlike now, communicating and keeping in touch with people in Fiji was not easy. At the time I was growing up in Fiji, there were no computers, Internet, cellular phones, and not everyone had a telephone in their homes. Only wealthy people were able to afford a telephone. Keeping up with friends outside of school was impossible due to the inability to communicate.

School break was over, and it was time to go back to school. This time was a little different than when I first started school. I was more confident and looked forward to being back in school. I was eager to meet new people and make friends, but I knew that no one could take the place of Satya. The new school was much more complicated. Instead of one teacher, I had several teachers now. I instantly made a few friends. From being a shy little girl, I was turning into a young, confident woman. One morning, I opened my desk to put my books in and found a note from a boy saying how beautiful I looked. Up until now, I was oblivious to dating since my mom and dad, my three brothers, and my sister had arranged marriages. Arranged marriage was an expectation in my culture, so dating someone before marriage was out of the question. I knew that one day my parents would find a match for me as it was the norm in my family. My friends and I made fun of that boy for leaving the note for me. That really embarrassed him. I felt bad about it later when I understood more about dating and love.

As I was growing up, the expectations from family were increasing as well. My dad asked me to help in his real estate business when I was not in school. Every weekend, I began helping my dad by answering the phone, setting up appointments, and filing papers. Some Saturdays, I was able to watch a movie in the movie theater with the friends I made at school and a couple of friends I made in the neighborhood. My life was enjoyable, and I had two years until high school graduation. One evening, dad announced at the dinner table that he was planning to move us to Vancouver, Canada. We all looked at each other, in shock, but did not say anything to my dad. My older sister, Prem, and her family lived there. Munna and I were the only ones moving with my parents. We spent the next several months preparing for the move. The last few months of preparation were very stressful, emotional, and draining. The thought of leaving my friends, brothers, cousins, and relatives was excruciating. My parents sold most of the things we had, or shared with my brothers since they were unable to relocate with us due to not meeting age requirements by Canadian immigration. My knowledge about the country I was moving to was minimal. There were no computers, so I could not research the place. My dad had told us that there were better opportunities for Munna and me. I also remembered my dad telling us how excited he was to see and feel the snow. After listening to my dad, I was eager to experience the snow, too. I had seen snow on postcards and Christmas cards. There was no television on the island, so everything was just imagination. It makes me sometimes laugh when imagining my dad's face talking about how excited he was to see and feel the snow, and here now, we pay thousands of dollars to go to tropical places to get away from snow. Thankfully, living in Florida, I don't have to deal with the cold winters, but before that, I had spent a fortune traveling to the Caribbean Islands to feel the island vibe and tropical environment. Well, I must say that once an island girl, you are always an island girl.

GOLDEN NUGGET

Sometimes when we feel that we have things under control, the road of life takes an unexpected turn and leaves you with no choice but to follow where the road takes you. Certain changes are necessary in life to help us grow.

CHAPTER THREE

Never Take Anything for Granted

*We can't be afraid of change. You may feel very
secure in the pond that you are in, but if you
never venture out of it, you will never know
that there is such a thing as an ocean, a sea.
Holding onto something that is good for you
now, may be the very reason why you
don't have something better.*

—C. JoyBell C.

After several months of preparation for the move, the day finally arrived on August 30, 1980. My cousins, relatives, older brothers, and neighbors gathered at our place to say our goodbyes to each other. My mom was crying upon departure, but she was trying hard to hide her feelings by working to smile and carry on a conversation with everyone. I saw her wiping her tears with a handkerchief when no one was watching. I truly understood the pain she was going through better when I became a mom and had to say goodbye to my kids. It is true that we tend to understand things better in life when we experience them ourselves. My mom knew that it was a long way to Canada from Fiji, and she didn't know if she would ever see her sons, parents, other relatives, or neighbors again. It took a four-hour ride on a bus to go from Suva to Nadi International Airport. Moving away from Fiji and heading to Vancouver, Canada was a big deal at that time. In preparation for the move, we all bought new outfits. We all had to look smashing when we landed in Vancouver, Canada. It's the first impression that counts.

My mom's outfit particularly stood out. She wore her favorite red saree with white embroidered flower design and sequins all over. Fearing cold, she wore her new black fur coat on top of her saree, which she bought in one of the local Fijian stores. Even to this day, I wonder why a store on an island in the South Pacific would sell a fur coat. It was not understandable at that time and still isn't. Regardless, she purchased one and wore it to Vancouver. My dad hired a bus driver to take everyone to the airport to say our final goodbye. It was normal at that time in Fiji for the entire family and friends to go to the airport for a final farewell. Munna and I then followed my mom. The flight attendant said to my mom as she walked on the plane wearing her fur coat, "Welcome aboard ma'am! It is too warm in Vancouver at the moment for that coat. It's summer right now. You may want to save that for winter!"

My mom was embarrassed from the comment, realizing immediately how secluded her life had been. Still, at the same time, she was innocently unaware of the immediate climate ahead in Vancouver. With these thoughts in mind, she did not respond verbally, but smiled and walked to her seat. This action spoke clearly of how she lived her life with humility and respect for others. Many things started to come to my mind. Will people judge me like the flight attendant appeared to judge my mom? The quick culture shock temporarily reduced my excitement for the trip.

Finally, we got settled in our seats on the plane. Munna, my older brother, had the window seat, and I sat next to him. The flight attendant went over the safety drill in English. I admired everything about the flight attendant and wanted to be just like her. Possibly, one day, I could become a flight attendant and be like her and travel the world. Maybe it was at that moment that my passion for traveling began and has never ended.

The plane started to roll on the runway, and I held tightly to the armrests, all the while making sure several times that my seat belt was securely tight. As the plane built up speed, my heartbeat sped up, faster and faster with a fear of the unknown. It was then that, while looking out the window, I saw the wings on the plane flexing. As usual, my brother Munna saw the scared look on my face and decided to scare me more by telling me the wings were flexing because there was something wrong with the plane, and it was about to crash. Not knowing anything about airplanes, it was natural for me to believe him. My dad saw me almost in tears, and then he told Munna to stop scaring me. I will never forget the moment my brother scared me on the plane. To this day, I still reflect on it whenever flying on an airplane, and laugh about it.

My brothers loved to scare me since I was little. As an aside, I clearly remember that, one day, one of my brothers brought me a small paper bag containing what he said was candy. The bag was heavy, so I expected a lot of sweets. My eyes got bigger with excitement when I saw the bag. My curiosity grew, and I quickly opened the bag, and a giant cane toad jumped out. In the next instant, I started screaming and running as fast as I could to get away. It was more like a life and death situation for me. I had no idea where I was going; I was just running down the hill toward the beach as fast as I could. Quite simply, I just wanted to get away from that toad. In the background, I could hear my brothers saying, "Vinnu, the toad is coming behind you to get you."

I finally stopped when I heard my dad shouting, "Vinnu come back. The toad is gone."

Ever since I can remember, I've had a phobia of toads, and my brothers fully understood and most likely were involved in the development of this irrational fear. To this day, many years later, I still have a phobia of toads. One night, when going home from work late, it was raining heavily. Our house in Virginia was built on a two-acre corner lot, with a creek right behind the house, which was heaven for toads. As I was getting out of my car around midnight, I saw three big toads sitting in front of my front door. Due to the location of the house, there was no way of going through the back door. So, there I was, sitting in my car for a few hours, waiting for the toads to leave. They were stubborn and decided not to move. Seeing their comfort level in staying put, I gave up and drove ten miles at one o'clock in the morning to a gas station to have breakfast. I finished eating at about two o'clock in the morning. I was tired from working all day. I decided to drive back, hoping to get into the house to sleep. Well, the toads chose to stay. My only option was to sleep in the car, which I did. Finally, I was able to get into my house at seven o'clock in the morning. Quite frankly, I still don't know why I am so terrified of toads. Could it be that my childhood experiences with my brothers have contributed to it? Regardless of the reason, people always make fun of my toad phobia. When I told my colleagues at work about my crazy and adventurous night, to my surprise, I was offered several accommodations at their homes in case the toads decided to barricade my door again!

After approximately fifteen hours of traveling, we finally landed in Vancouver, Canada, not knowing what was next. We could only imagine what it would be like based on what dad said and what we saw on Christmas cards or postcards that generally portrayed an abundance of snow everywhere. We all got off the plane with our new and exclusive dressed-to-impress outfits. It took a couple of hours before we got done with immigration. After picking up our luggage—and I mean lots of luggage—I finally saw my sister Prem standing and desperately waiting for us. She hugged my mom and dad, and they all cried with joy. My sister is the eldest sibling, and she got married and left home when I was only three years old. She lived in England with her husband for five years after marriage. She returned briefly to Fiji before moving to Vancouver, Canada, not giving enough time for me to get to know her or develop the closeness siblings usually have. The age gap between us was another huge factor. Due to the significant age difference, I wasn't as close to my sister as I was to my brothers. She looked so much like my mom, similar height and build, facial features, curly hair, and smile. She came and kissed Munna and me on the cheeks, and said that she was glad to have us in Vancouver, Canada. We all got our luggage, boxes, and bags, and then walked to her minivan, which had three rows of seat that could seat up to eight people. We all thought that the minivan was so cool as we didn't have that in Fiji. We stood for a moment and looked around. Of all of us, the look on my dad's face was priceless. It was almost as if he had won a lottery. Vancouver was nothing that we had imagined. It was a warm, sunny day with blue sky like Fiji, minus the coconut palms. It was easy to see the confused look on my mom's face. She looked at my sister and exclaimed, "Where is all the snow? I was under the impression that it would be freezing here."

To make matters even funnier, she was still holding on to her fur coat. My sister then explained to us all about the four seasons in Vancouver. Suddenly, we had a better understanding of what the flight attendant meant.

There are specific experiences in life I still remember, and this is one of them. We were content and excited as we looked out the windows in the van that my sister was driving. There were so many roads, cars, tall buildings, beautiful trees, flowers, and, of course, people dressed in shorts and t-shirts. Unlike in Fiji where young girls wore either a dress or jeans, older women a traditional saree or mumu (long dress), and men shorts or sulu, a kilt-like outfit. It was so different from what I was used to, which included coconut palms, white sandy beaches, mango trees, papaya trees, and banana trees, to mention a few. Suddenly, I started missing the Fiji Islands. Why did we have to give up the things we loved? Life is not fair sometimes, but it's all about accepting, adjusting, appreciating, and living in the moment.

We finally arrived at my sister's house. It was a two-level basement house with three bedrooms, two bathrooms, and a living room. My sister, my brother-in-law, their two kids, and my sister's mother-in-law were living in the house. We all had to somehow accommodate ourselves on the main floor as someone else was renting the basement. It was kind of awkward, but again, life is all about adjusting to the situation in the moment.

That night my sister held a welcoming party for us. We got to meet many relatives that we did not know and got to try many different food dishes. My sister had prepared it all by herself. She was an excellent cook, like my mom. In my sister's house, I noticed that men and women did not sit or eat together. The men were singing Fijian songs in the living room while the women were chitchatting in the kitchen. The dinner table setup was different for me. We always ate together as a family. This utterly different experience made me miss the family time we had back in Fiji. It is true that in life you don't realize what you have until it's gone.

The next morning, my sister made some pancakes for us. It was the first time I got to try pancakes with lots of butter and syrup. They were amazing. Every once in a while, when eating pancakes, it takes me back to my first pancake experience. It's the little things in life that make us smile. My sister was an amazing woman, just like my mom. She worked full time as a nurse, looked after the home, and took care of her children, mother-in-law, and now us! It would have been nice to have her with us in Fiji growing up. Although much older, she could have been the sister with whom to share secrets, play dolls, and do girly stuff. Instead, I grew up with my five brothers, who taught me how to play ball, climb trees, catch fish, and, of course, box. My brothers had a punching bag in the one of the spare rooms in our house in Fiji and included me while they practiced boxing. They taught me how to punch and defend myself. It's funny, despite all the self-defense lessons I got from my brothers, I was never able to use them in real life. My sister was a strong and hardworking woman like my mom. She was very gentle, giving, and caring. She never raised her voice to anyone, not even her kids. She seemed more like my mom than my sister. During the next couple of weeks, we got to know my sister, brother-in-law, niece, and nephew, and my sister's mother-in-law. We were also introduced to the house rules. My sister enrolled me in school, which was three miles away. Distinctly, I remember my sister and parents telling me that night, "Vinnu, you have to work hard in school. It will be different from what you are used to."

Testing by the school was necessary to determine my initial grade level. The night before the test was very nerve-racking for me, thinking, *what if I don't pass? What if I have to go back a grade? What will people say?* Being a tenacious person since childhood, I was determined to pass this test, and I did. I moved up a class based on my test scores, which meant that I would graduate in two years instead of three. Woo-hoo! Things were finally falling in place for me. Regardless, I still deeply missed my home in Fiji, my brothers, my friends, and my past easygoing lifestyle. But there was no turning back now, and indeed I had to keep going. Occasionally, I cried when alone. Soon, I learned to live in the moment, enjoy what life had to offer, and how to make the most of it.

It was precisely a month after the move when I started school. My sister drove me to school the first few days, and then I learned the way and walked back and forth from home to school. Everything was so different in the new school. They gave us each a locker to put all of our books in, and we had to change classrooms. In Fiji, teachers went to diverse classrooms, whereas in Vancouver, the students had to change classrooms. There was a lot to learn. Again, life is all about adjusting and accepting changes.

In Vancouver, fall was all about leaves changing colors from green to orange, yellow, and red. It was enjoyable looking at the leaves changing colors as I walked to school every day. Everything about nature and the outdoors has always amazed me. The world is such a beautiful place. The school in Vancouver was not a piece of cake; it was challenging, but soon I made a few friends in school. It felt like a majority of the students thought I was a dork and didn't want to have anything to do with me. It is easy to feel like an outcast, freshly off the boat. We didn't have all the fancy stuff that others had. To make matters worse, I occasionally wore my island clothes to school. Our property in Fiji still had not sold, so we didn't have much money, and this did not help matters. We were all trying to survive with what we brought from our home in Fiji. Guess what? The day finally arrived when my dad experienced what he had envisioned for Vancouver, and for the very first time in our lives, we saw the ground and trees covered in snow. Running to my mom and dad, I exclaimed, "Mom, Dad, run, look outside, it's snowing."

We all went outside to experience the snow. It was a strange feeling, as a few months ago I only saw snow in pictures or on postcards, and now I was touching it. It was easy to see the excitement on my dad's face when he saw and felt the snow. It looked like he was about to cry with joy. It was nice to see my mom and dad happy.

My mom and dad's first snow experience in Vancouver, Canada

We all knew that they were struggling in this strange, new place, but they did not want to admit it to my brother and me. Not having much knowledge about the snow, I assumed that it was okay for me to walk to school in my sneakers. Grabbing my mom's umbrella, I wore my only jacket, and sneakers from

Fiji, and started walking to school. Well, things were not as simple as I thought they would be. My umbrella broke due to snow piling on top of it, and my shoes filled with snow, which made me miss school. It was so disappointing to miss a school day due to inappropriate outerwear and footwear. With help and instructions from my sister, we built a huge snowman the next day. Life is, indeed, full of surprises. Not too long before, I was playing on the beach, making a sandcastle, and today I was building a snowman. Life is so unpredictable. You never know what is ahead of you. It is important to live your life to the fullest every day. Appreciate the little things in life as there are no guarantees.

After a few months, my dad went back to Fiji to sell our property. My mom was able to find a job as a nursing assistant in Vancouver. My brother, Munna, also found a career as a draftsperson. In a few months, the basement became available at my sister's house, so she and my brother-in-law asked us to rent the basement from them. The little money my mom and brother made at that time barely covered the rent, utilities, and food. We couldn't afford a car, so we learned to either walk or take public transportation. It broke my heart to see my mom getting ready every night to ride the bus to her fulltime job, while also having to take care of us kids. My mom was tired all the time but never gave up or lost hope. It was apparent that she missed her life in Fiji but she never complained. We were lucky that Vancouver had good public transportation. The struggle continued until my dad sold our place in Fiji.

Sometimes, you just have to bow your head, say a prayer, and weather the storm.

—Anonymous

After six months of trying, our property sold, and my dad returned to Vancouver. We were now able to move into a much bigger place, which was a rental property. We could finally see the light at the end of the tunnel. My dad also got a job in the post office, sorting mail. During my school break, I helped as much as I could by doing odd jobs like picking berries on a farm and also working in the post office, sorting mail as needed. Our new place was much closer to the school, so the walk was much shorter. In about a year, my dad bought a house. It was a beautiful, three-story house built on a hill. It had an excellent view of Mount Baker, which I loved. The backyard was ample in size. The yard contained a garden with flowers and vegetables, allowing us to harvest fresh, organic vegetables, and to plant flowers. Unlike Fiji, there weren't any hibiscuses, gardenias, or plumerias, but instead, our flower garden had beautiful azaleas, daffodils, and tulips. Life goes faster when you have purpose in life. In the blink of an eye, it was time for me to graduate from high school. It seemed like just yesterday I started school. This was first time that my parents were attending a graduation ceremony. Munna graduated in Fiji, and there wasn't any graduation ceremony for graduate students there at that time. My parents took me shopping for a graduation dress. After a few weeks of looking, I finally found the dress I liked. It was a long, baby blue, pleated dress. My parents were standing by the fitting room, waiting eagerly to see me in that dress. I saw the same sparkle on my parents' faces when I used to stand in front of them with a new dress when I was a little girl. The day of graduation finally arrived, and I walked on the stage wearing my blue dress to the graduation theme song,I didn't think much of that song until later in life.

Sailing takes me away to where I've always heard it could be, just a dream and the wind to carry me. And soon, I will be free.

—CHRISTOPHER CROSS

My high school graduation.1982, at David Thompson Secondary school, Vancouver, Canada

Each word in that song was so true to our journey in life. Everyone clapped as I received my high school diploma. My parents were incredibly proud of me. I felt a sense of accomplishment. The transition in school from Fiji to Vancouver, Canada was challenging, but my hard work finally paid off. I graduated with a high GPA. I learned not to give up in life—not to *ever* give up. Every experience, whether good or bad, teaches us something. There's always a sunrise after every sunset. Perseverance is the key!

> *Life is about accepting the challenges along the way, choosing to keep moving forward, and savoring the journey.*
>
> —ROY T. BENNETT

After finishing high school, it was time to face the real world. Unlike other students, I had not thought about going to college and did not have any future goals. Several times, my dad suggested that I should consider nursing as a career, just as my mom and sister had. It did not impress me at that time, but instead, I chose to become a hairdresser. After seven months of attending hairdressing school, I got a real job in a high-end salon in downtown Vancouver. I worked for about a year as a hairdresser in the city of Vancouver. It gave me a little glimpse of the life of a single person in a big city. It was good while it lasted.

GOLDEN NUGGET

Every experience in life, whether it's good or bad, takes us one step closer to where we belong. Life experiences shape us into who we become.

CHAPTER FOUR

Buried Under Cultural Burden

*Don't let the expectations and opinions of other
people affect your decisions. It's your life, not
theirs. Do what matters most to you; do what
makes you feel alive and happy. Don't let the
expectations and ideas of others limit who you
are. If you let others tell you who you are, you
are living their reality — not yours. There is
more to life than pleasing people. There is much
more to life than following others' prescribed
path. There is so much more to life than what
you experience right now. You need to decide
who you are for yourself. Become a
whole being. Adventure.*

—Roy T. Bennett

C ultural expectations can sometimes obligate us
to do things in life, even if we disagree. Arranged
marriages have been a part of Indian culture since
the fourth century. There are many aspects to be considered

when choosing a match; for example, religion, values and beliefs, education, caste, social and financial status, and of course, family background. The caste system is a social structure that divides different groups into rank categories. Members of the higher caste cannot marry members of the lower caste. Marriage is arranged by the family to keep that social structure. I belonged to the uppermost caste, so the match had to be from the highest caste as well. Since my great grandparents were from India, they practiced their cultural beliefs in Fiji too.

Arranged marriages weave families together according to the Indian culture. It's not just about husband and wife; it's like marrying the entire family. It's usually a long process where both sides of the family are typically in contact with each other and approve the marriage before the bride and groom can meet and talk themselves. They only do that to get acquainted before the actual ceremony. In other words, what the potential bride and groom like or dislike does not matter. At present, many in the contemporary generation believe in love first, whereas arranged marriages are just the opposite. In arranged marriages, marriage is first, and then it is expected the two people will fall in love over time. Although I found it to be bizarre, at the same time, I have always been someone who respects my cultural beliefs. There were things in life that I desired above and beyond the predetermined and confined arranged marriage. Although I was born and raised in Fiji, my family and I continued to follow the tenets, beliefs, and precepts of Hinduism. It was an expectation that I marry someone my family would choose for me. Arranged marriages were still common in Fiji at that time. Living in Vancouver at age nineteen, my family expected me to fly to Fiji and get married. My family chose my future husband based on the edicts of ensuring the same religion and caste. Even with fear-based reservations, ultimately, I would have to marry the person of my family's choosing. As an Indian girl, I was excited about wearing a beautiful, traditional Indian wedding dress and having a traditional Indian wedding.

Additionally, I dreamt of having a house of my own and of bearing children. Occasionally, I did wonder if people fell in love with their spouses in an arranged marriage. More realistically, the real question was whether the prearranged marriage was more for the family's benefit or mine. If you ended up falling in love after the ceremony, it was a bonus. Social structure has priority and one's individual choice and happiness are secondary. In preparation for the wedding ceremony, I spent a few months shopping in Vancouver. Once completed, it was time to meet my future husband, Birju. Up to that point in time, I had only seen his picture. With excitement and trepidation, I finally arrived in Fiji, and my brother Yogi picked me up at the airport. It had been three or four years since I left Fiji for Vancouver, so both Yogi and I were excited to see each other. Many memories came back as I looked out the window as my brother drove us to his home. Things were a little different now. Now, after getting used to Western culture, I was expected to come back to the place I had to leave without being given a choice. All of a sudden, I started feeling homesick for Vancouver as that was my home now. The car finally arrived at my brother Yogi's place, and my sister-in-law Nita came out of their small one-bedroom apartment to welcome me. My brother informed me that my future husband's family, without my future husband, would be coming to meet me that evening, and I had to cook a few dishes so they could taste my cooking. In all fairness, why doesn't the family of the bride get to evaluate the groom's handiness, intelligence, and overall worthiness? Culturally, I know why, but how was I expected to cook and entertain at age nineteen after traveling for over fifteen hours from Vancouver?

That evening, almost ten family members of my future family, except my future husband, came to meet me. His whole family had to approve the arranged marriage before I met him. An appropriate outfit was essential to get approval from my future husband's side of the family for our arranged marriage. For the formal interview, I wore a traditional Indian outfit called a saree. A saree is an exquisite outfit made from five meters of decorated fabric and wrapped around a blouse and skirt. As expected, I was supposed to serve my future mother-in-law and sisters-in-law as it was against the culture for the brothers-in-law to ever see the bride's face. Ever. By tradition, I made an Indian tea called chai and a sweet called halwa. It is a traditional dish made with semolina, clarified butter, sugar, and milk. The expectation is for the future bride to cook, so the groom's family can evaluate her cooking ability. Fortunately for me, and to avert potential embarrassment, I learned cooking when I was twelve, helping my mom in the kitchen.

Distinctly, I still remember walking in my saree with a serving tray loaded with tea and halwa for everyone. In my culture, serving sweets was considered good luck and helped to solidify the bonds between people. Everyone's eyes were stuck on me as I walked in front of them. True to tradition, I said, "namaste," (hello) with my hands together in front of my face, bowing my head forward in submission and respect to each individual one-by-one, purposely starting with my future mother-in-law. Being introverted,

I reserved my words to answer their questions. After tea, sweets, and greetings came the main meal, which I served to the family. Tradition dictates that the bride-to-be serves the family first, and once finished, eats afterward. They all loved the dishes I cooked, which was a great sign.

Before leaving that night, my mother-in-law gave me forty Fijian dollars, which in my culture means that she was happy with me and accepted me as her future daughter-in-law. My future mother-in-law was engaging me to her son, and I was to leave all the other boys alone. In the next few days, both sides of the family arranged for my future husband and me to meet for lunch and get acquainted with each other. Oddly enough, since up to this point I had only seen his picture, I kept wondering if he looked the same. My brother dropped me off at the restaurant, and I saw my future husband-to-be, Birju, in person, standing in front of the restaurant, for the first time. A strange feeling overcame me when I saw Birju as he was the man I would marry in a month. What if I didn't like him? Although it was not natural or comfortable, I controlled my feelings and said to myself that my family knows him, so I shouldn't worry. He came up to me, introduced himself, and shook my hand. We spent a few hours at the restaurant eating and getting to know each other. The lunch date went well. He was very kind and attentive to me. He offered to show me around the city, and then he dropped me off at my brother's place. It was kind of nice to be able to see him and talk in person before the wedding as this was not always the case in arranged Indian marriages. Do not be mistaken. This was not a romantic date but a way to maintain social status in my caste. The wedding had to be expedited due to being pressed for time to get back to Vancouver. The next few weeks were hectic, preparing for the wedding. It was up to my family to find a temple and a priest to perform the wedding. There were invitations to send out beforehand and food to prepare every day, along with decorations and flowers to be purchased and placed. Hindu wedding ceremonies usually take about four to five days, including a henna design ceremony, turmeric ceremony, and a ceremony of family coming together.

Finally, the wedding day arrived. My parents weren't able to attend the wedding from Canada, so my brother Yogi was the one to give me away. It was a bittersweet day for me. I missed my parents, especially my dad, as I had always dreamt that my dad would be the one giving me away. The dress for a traditional Indian wedding included a red saree with a red veil and lots of gold jewelry. My hair was professionally styled with painstaking effort to incorporate white flowers. Next, came the henna design ceremony. My brother Yogi hired a lady to apply the henna on both of my hands and feet. Many of my relatives came to the wedding, but I missed my parents as they could not take time off from work in Vancouver. Occasionally, I have reflected back on when my parents used to say that they never wanted to give me away in marriage. Was that the reason for them not attending my wedding?

My wish would have been for my dad to be there to see his youngest daughter, his princess, in her wedding dress. There were relatives and family friends there that I had not seen in years. When sitting on the floor in a little, decorated room in the temple, in my bridal outfit, I suddenly heard someone yelling, "The (Baraat) procession has arrived."

Wedding day, in my bridal outfit, sitting on the floor of the Temple.

The groom came in a decorated car with friends and family to the wedding, called a procession. Butterflies were flying in my stomach. It was the excitement all girls get when they fall in love, but for me, it was also the feelings of uncertainty, otherwise known as cold feet. My sister-in-law, Nita, and a few other female relatives came into my room with a basket wrapped in yellow cloth. They opened the basket in front of me. The contents included jewelry and clothes purchased and offered by my future husband. Nita, with help from the other women, placed the necklace around my neck. It was a tradition that I wear the jewelry given by my future husband during the ceremony.

The groom arrived with his family and met my sister-in-law, Nita, and other female relatives at the doorway. They received him with gifts as part of a welcome ceremony. After that, the groom's family took him to the ceremonial area. At that point, Nita and other female relatives took me to the ceremony area. He was standing waiting for me where the ceremony was supposed to take place. For only the second time, I saw my future husband. My soon-to-be husband and I exchanged garlands made with fresh flowers as per tradition and walked around the sacred fire together. There were seven rounds, (phere) with us saying a separate vow (sapat) with each. With each round, we stopped and prayed to God and made the following promises to each other:

First Round —to nourish each other

Second Round —to grow together; mentally, physically and spiritually

Third —to preserve our wealth and prosperity

Fourth —to serve each other in happiness and harmony

Fifth —to care for our health and our long-lived children

Sixth —to be together forever in all responsibilities

Seventh —to have everlasting friendship and true companionship.

Directly after the completion of the seven rounds, the sindoor (red powder) was applied by the groom to my forehead. My brother Yogi, and my sister-in-law Nita, gave me away since my parents were not there. After this, we were pronounced husband and wife by the priest. Instead of going to my husband Birju's house, we all stayed at the temple that night as it was considered bad luck to go to the groom's house on the wedding night. It seemed like a long night, sleeping on the floor of that small room in the temple. Nita and a few other female relatives slept in the same room I was in. My husband slept in another room with his family. The next morning, I went to my husband's place. There was a bridal welcoming ceremony, and then I returned to my brother Yogi's house for few days until final departure from his house to Birju's house. It was time for me to gather all my belongings. From this point forward, my husband's house was considered my permanent home. My family had told me that once married, my husband's home would be my home, and I was not supposed to ever leave his place and return to my parents' house. Tradition would have it that the only time I would leave his home was when I was dead.

All of a sudden, the excitement of newly married life was gone. It was a gut-wrenching feeling I felt, like I was losing myself and becoming someone or something else. What about my dreams and desires? Would I ever have a chance to do things that I wanted to do in life?

After a few days of being at my brother Yogi's house, Birju and his family came to pick me up and take me to his place, forever. Yogi, Nita, and a few other relatives were there to say goodbye to me. Everyone was crying as I headed to my husband Birju's car. It was strange that no matter what life brought, I was never to leave Birju's house and come back, but yet everyone was crying because I was going. Some things I never understood and will never understand. It was about a twenty minute drive to Birju's house. That night, there was another bridal welcoming party for fifty people. Next, I found out, after getting there, that a newlywed bride was required to cook for the guests. It was a ritual that the bride cooks, and that guests taste the food and give money if it's good. Luckily, my mother-in-law helped me in the kitchen, cooking and cleaning before and after the party. She was an amazing woman, and I could see in her eyes that she had gone through exactly what I was going through. It was indeed was a bonding time for us. We became very close to each other.

That night was my honeymoon. It was around midnight when everyone finally left. It was at this point I was finally able to go to bed, after washing dishes and cleaning the kitchen. Finally, Birju and I would have intimate one-on-one time. Although we did have a great time together the day we first met, it felt bizarre to be with him alone in one room, sharing a bed. Why did it feel so weird? Was that how love was supposed to feel? There was no opportunity to date before my marriage, so I didn't know how love between a man and a woman felt like. There was no passion between us, but I knew that he was my husband, and I was supposed to take care of him.

Moreover, I had a responsibility to serve his family temporarily, and spend the rest of my life with him. The next few weeks, we spent visiting all his family, and then cooking and cleaning as my husband returned to work a few days after the wedding. It was time for me to return home to Vancouver, Canada.

Relationships based on obligation lack dignity.

—Dr. Wayne Dyer

Finally, with much relief, I returned to my parents' home in Vancouver. Birju stayed back in Fiji as I had to complete sponsorship through immigration for him to join me in Vancouver. My parents were excited to see me again. Life felt normal after I returned to my parents. Everything felt like it was just a dream. Now being married, my parents' home was only a temporary residence for me. Soon after arrival, I called my boss to find out that the business where I worked as a hairdresser had closed, leaving me with no job. It was difficult for me to get another job right away, as I did not go to college after graduating from high school. I wished that I would have listened to my dad and enrolled in the nursing program instead of being hard-headed and entering the cosmetology program. Sometimes we become rebellious, thinking our parents are trying to control our lives by trying to tell us what to do, when in reality, parents try to guide us in the right direction. My parents were very supportive and told me that I could live with them until I could find a good job and manage to live on my own. After the completion of the immigration paperwork, my husband joined me in Vancouver.

My parents organized a reception party for us after he arrived. Like any other girl would be, I was excited about the reception party. My relatives and friends from school helped me to choose a reception outfit—a beautiful silver and gray saree with matching jewelry. I had my hair styled with white and silver flowers. My husband wore a dark blue suit. We both looked great together.

Everyone was having a great time, and my husband and I danced together for the very first time. He had a few drinks, and I had a few glasses of champagne. Distinctly, I remember sitting with my family, drinking champagne while he was drinking and socializing with a few guys. My school girlfriend's husband came and asked me to dance. At that point, there was no reason for me to believe there was anything wrong with dancing with him as we all were good friends. Shortly after we began dancing, I saw Birju rushing angrily toward me all of a sudden. He grabbed my hand and took me outside the hall.

He started yelling at me. "Vinnu, why did you dance with another man?"

I said, "He is simply and only my friend's husband."

For the very first time, I saw deep and irrational anger on his face. The problem was his drinking. He became an abusive and unreasonable person, especially toward me since he thought he owned me. He grabbed and lifted me as I was crying and screaming. There was a tree stump. He dropped me forcefully on the stump. I closed my eyes and felt pain in my back. He pulled me off the stump and dropped me on the ground and kicked me on my side. While lying on the ground, I opened my eyes and saw my brother and his friends looking at me and trying to calm Birju down while he was cursing at everyone.

Birju told my parents, "Keep your daughter, I don't want her anymore."

My parents begged him to calm down. Being in severe pain, I went home crying and could not sleep that night. The next day, I told my parents and family I didn't want to be with him. Sons-in-law were considered higher than any other family member, so my family got very angry with me as it was a disgrace, and divorce was simply unacceptable, regardless of circumstances. Quickly, my family reminded me I could only leave him when I was deceased.

I have often wondered what my life would have been like if I was able to leave Birju after the first physical beating? But then I would not have my two beautiful children, Erin and Moni. To that end, everything in life has its purpose.

Months passed, and he continued to drink, and create issues with my family and me. Additionally, I also found out in those months that I was pregnant with my first child, Erin. Here we were, with no jobs, expecting our first child. I was happy that I would become a mom but sad that I still was unemployed. My parents were very supportive and told me not to worry about anything. I could see how happy they were about having a grandchild from their youngest child. At age twenty, I had my first child. Delivering naturally, labor lasted almost thirty-six hours, with intense pain. The experience of having a baby was the best thing at that time. He was beautiful, with lots of dark hair, dark eyes, and tan colored skin. He was just perfect. Now I had purpose in life. It was hard to believe that I was a mom. While nursing Erin, a special bond developed between us. It was a deep, close feeling I had never experienced before.

Frequently, I found myself looking at him and thinking about how beautiful he was. After a few days in the hospital, it was finally time to go home. It took a while to recover from the trauma of thirty-six hours of labor. Mom's help was much needed post labor and delivery. As per tradition, my mom hired a lady to take care of the baby and me for a few days while I was recovering. It was customary in my culture to have someone take care of new moms after delivery. My mom prepared a drink for me made with milk, ginger, and other spices to increase milk production. The lady she hired gave me a full body massage every day. It was supposed to help heal the body and, indeed, it helped. I was not aware of the benefits of massage and relaxation therapy at that time. Everything made sense later in life when I became a nurse by profession, and taught my patients the benefits of relaxation therapy and its healing effects.

Days passed by. Erin was growing up, but neither of us had jobs. We were living with my parents on the savings I had in the bank and the little bit of money Birju brought. My parents helped us as much as they could while I was looking for another job. Birju was a welder by trade, but his certification was not valid or recognized in Vancouver, Canada. He did some odd jobs here and there but not enough for us to find our own place. Erin was six months old when my brother Yogi and sister-in-law Nita came to visit us. My dad arranged dinner at my parents' house and invited a few of our relatives. My dad, Birju, Yogi, and Munna were drinking alcohol and having a good time. My mom and I were in the kitchen preparing dinner for everyone.

Suddenly, I heard yelling and screaming. My dad and Birju had started arguing. Birju started cursing at my dad, and that's when my dad told him to leave the house for good. It was around ten o'clock at night. Full of anger, Birju ran upstairs and started gathering all of our things. Although

I did not want to leave the house with my six-month-old son, I was told by my family to go with my husband. Not knowing what life had ahead of me, I gathered my things as I was told and left the house with Birju and Erin at night. At that point, we had neither jobs nor money. Would there be a time when I would be able to make my own decisions in life? Only time would tell.

Birju and I, along with Erin, took shelter at one of our relative's house for a few days. They helped us find a small and inexpensive one-bedroom basement suite for us. Our relatives paid the rent for the first month. We did not have money for a continuing lease. The landlord would kick the door and mentally, but not physically, harass me every day when Birju was away. I distinctly remember not coming out of the basement suite, fearing that the landlord would confront me about the rent. Hiding inside the basement suite with my son became the norm for me. I tried to give the best to Erin with what little we had by preparing all his baby food at home. He loved mashed banana and rice cereal. There were uncountable days when we stayed hungry so that we could feed Erin. Indeed, every situation in life teaches us something. I learned from all this that you should never take anything for granted in life. Things can change in the blink of an eye.

In a few weeks, with help from one of our relatives, Birju got a job in a bakery, temporarily. At this point, I was still a stay-at-home mom, taking care of my son. It was the second month after moving out of my parents' place when my dad ended up having a heart attack. I remember clearly, while breastfeeding Erin, Yogi, my brother, came to my home to tell me about our dad. Immediately, I burst into tears as I was always my dad's princess and very close to him. With all the problems between Birju and my dad, I was told by Birju to never, ever contact or see my dad. Yogi said to me that my dad had been asking for me and wanted to see me. Birju was at work at that time, and I did not think twice as to what the outcome would be if he found out that I went to see my dad without his permission. For the first time, I saw my dad in a hospital bed, hooked up to oxygen and tubes. He looked very pale and sick. He started crying when he saw me. We both cried, and I sat beside him for a long time that day. Once Birju found out I was visiting my dad, he was furious and told Yogi that he didn't want me back as I had disobeyed him. My family, and in particular Yogi, begged him to take me back once again. Some things in life don't change. It was evident that there was no love between Birju and me. The question was: would I be able to survive and continue living a life like this? Evidently, my son was the only reason for me to continue this marriage.

Love and compassion are necessities, not luxuries.
Without them humanity cannot survive.

—DALAI LAMA

Eventually, after being in the hospital for a few weeks, my dad recovered and went home. My life with Birju and Erin continued as usual, and I was not allowed to see or visit my dad for a long time.

There were times when I was scared for my life but had no choice but to stay due to cultural obligations. For instance, one of Birju's brothers was visiting us from Fiji for a week. One night, a few days before his brother was supposed to go back to Fiji, Birju planned on having few drinks with his brother. They both drank, but Birju did not stop until the bottle of Johnnie Walker was finished, which was around six o'clock in the morning. After eating breakfast, his brother left the house to visit other relatives.

It was about eleven o'clock and Birju was still awake, talking to me about his family in Fiji and how he wanted to send them something back with his brother. I said to him, "We still have lots of time. We can go shopping for your family before your brother leaves."

I saw the anger on his face as he looked at me. He got up from the kitchen chair, where he was sitting while Erin was in the playpen and I was washing dishes. He exclaimed, "Get ready. We are going shopping now."

I turned around to face him and said, "How can we go shopping when you are so drunk? You can't drive. It will put all of us at risk."

We had a Mini Cooper at that time. Although I did have a driver's license, I couldn't drive because our car was a standard shift, not an automatic. He rushed angrily to the kitchen drawer and pulled out a kitchen knife. I saw him coming toward me with the knife. The look on his face made me shiver. I had no time to think. He grabbed me by one side of my neck and placed the knife against the other, looking straight into my eyes. My tears did not have any impact on him.

He yelled, "Get ready now, or else I will slash your throat."

Fearing for my life, I obeyed his orders and got in the car, taking Erin with me, who was about a year old. Luckily, the mall was not too far from our house. Birju gave me an hour to buy things for his family at the mall. Erin was sleeping in his car seat, so he told me that he would watch Erin while I went into the mall. I shopped as fast as I could.

Upon returning to the car, I found Erin crying and Birju fast asleep in the driver's seat. I knocked on the window to wake Birju up since the car was locked. I had no choice but to call the police. The police opened the door and asked me to take Erin to my parents' house. Without thinking about what Birju would say if I went to my parents' house, I called my parents and went to their house. Birju came to my parents' house after a few days, apologizing for his behavior and, once again, I was told by my family to go back to Birju.

Life continued and now I was pregnant with my second child, Moni. Finally, I was able to get a part-time job in a store, organizing cards, and Birju got a fulltime job as a helper in a welding shop. One night, my friend invited us to her house for dinner. At that moment in time, I was six months pregnant with my first daughter, Moni. My husband had many beers with my friend's husband. We all had a great time until it was time to go home.

Erin was sleeping on my shoulder, ready to leave, when Birju looked at me angrily and said, "Vinnu, get my shoes and put them on."

Quickly, I looked at him and said, "I can't as I am holding Erin."

Angrily, he got up from the sofa, picked up his shoes, and hit me across my face while my friend and her husband watched. It was a very hurtful and embarrassing moment for me, and I cried for days, wondering if I should live my life like this. Expecting Moni, I felt helpless. How would I ever support two kids as a single mom? My feeling of helplessness held me in a limbo of sorts, and I went on with my life, hoping things would change one day. Finally, the day came when I gave birth to Moni. She was so beautiful, fair with lots of dark hair. She was a bundle of joy.

Moni was six months old when I went back to working part-time. One of our relatives agreed to help with babysitting. My parents occasionally called me or came to see me when Birju wasn't around. Things between Birju and my parents began to calm down a little, but I still wasn't allowed to visit my parents at their house. The physical abuse at home continued, and by now, it became the norm in our relationship. As a direct consequence, I decided to take my dad's advice and go back to college to pursue a career as a licensed practical nurse. Moni was about 2 years old and Erin was about 4 years old when I enrolled in a practical nursing program. To pay my tuition and help with the bills at home, I worked as a short-order cook in two restaurants. Birju did not like me going to school, so there were numerous times he would get drunk and throw my schoolwork away. My thoughts are that he did not want me getting my independence. As a result, I remember having to do my college nursing assignments when he wasn't home. It was a massive accomplishment for me when I graduated from my program and got my first real job. Never give up despite the obstacles in your life. Always believe in yourself that you can do it, and you will.

Live the Life of Your Dreams: Be brave enough to live the life of your dreams according to your vision and purpose instead of the expectations and opinions of others.

—Roy T. Bennett

Finally, I was able to earn decent money working as a licensed practical nurse. Working in a hospital enabled me to buy things for my kids that I wasn't able to buy before. Interestingly enough, my father had recommended I take this exact route many years before, but I never listened. Sometimes, our parents know us better than we know ourselves. Hardheadedness can lead to hardship at times. After a substantial delay, I followed his advice. We were now able to purchase a much bigger house. It always bothered me not having a say in my own home. Despite being the only one working fulltime in the house, I was still not allowed the freedom to have a separate bank account. Due to my fear of Birju hitting me, and wanting to save my marriage, I had to sign my checks, and allow Birju to deposit them in the joint checking account, only taking out a sparse weekly allowance for me.

Several years went by, and the physical and mental abuse continued. My kids witnessed it at times as well. There were many times I walked out on him for a good reason, but my parents and my family continued to guilt-talk me into going back with him.

Birju would then laugh at me and say, "See? No matter what I do to you, your family will always send you back to me."

What a brutal reality! I remember clearly one night when we went to watch the fireworks competition held every year in Vancouver. We went to Queen Elizabeth Park for a cookout. A few of Birju's friends joined us in the park. Erin and Moni started playing with the other kids. It was great to see everyone enjoying the park. Then, dreadfully, I saw Birju drinking with his friends, and I started fearing the worst. It was time to watch fireworks, and the park began to get crowded. There was a concrete bulkhead in the park to prevent people from falling. The park was on a hill, and it was a perfect place for people to stand and watch the fireworks. Standing behind the bulkhead, I was holding Moni in my arm, and Erin was standing by himself, holding my hand to watch the fireworks.

The fireworks were about to begin when all of a sudden, I heard Birju saying with a slurred speech, "Vinnu, stand on the bulkhead with the kids so they can see fireworks better."

Turning around, I said, "I can't stand on the bulkhead holding the kids because we will all fall and get hurt."

I saw that same deep, even, dark anger on his face as he looked at me. He angrily told me to go to the car with the kids. Obeying him, I took the kids to the car. He then told me to get in the car with the kids, and he was going to drive back home. He was drunk. It made no sense to put myself and our kids in danger by getting in that car. At that moment, he lost it. He punched me on the side of my face while Erin, Moni, and his friends watched, and grabbed my blouse and started to drag me down the parking lot. Both my kids started crying loudly, and he finally stopped. Then one of his friends came and offered to take me to my parents' place. Being in shock and scared, I quickly took the gracious offer and left the park with Erin and Moni. The very next day, despite my family telling me otherwise, I went to my family doctor. After arriving at the doctor's office, they evaluated the injuries I sustained from him punching me and dragging me. Going to my doctor was the best thing I did. He examined me and gave me some medication for the bruises. Luckily, the injuries weren't serious. My family doctor had a long talk with me that day that changed my thought process.

Vividly, I still remember him telling me, "Vinnu, it's time for you to start thinking about yourself and your children.

It is not good to bring children up in an abusive environment. They will grow up to believe that abuse is the norm."

He continued. "Vinnu, if any physical abuse happens more than once, chances are it will continue. I don't want to see you in my office with the same issue when you are fifty years old. You have your entire life ahead of you."

That was the best advice I ever got; it gave me the strength to move forward with my life. After all the years of taking physical and verbal abuse from Birju, I finally decided to file a report with the authorities and press charges against him, despite my family attempting to stop me. Over the next few weeks, my husband begged my family and me to drop the charges against him. My family kept pressuring me to drop the charges and go back with him. Incredibly, I listened to my family one more time and dropped those charges against him. He still had to appear in front of the judge. He was put on probation for six months and ordered to attend anger management classes. He continued to insist that he wanted the kids and me back, and promised that he would never be violent again. Well, like all the other times, I went back with him. Things were a little different now; he quit his job and stayed home with the kids. I continued to work fulltime. He was mentally abusive. He demanded that I cook when I got home at midnight from the evening shift. He would also invite his friends over and tell me to prepare a meal for everyone. One night, I came home and saw him drinking and smoking while my kids were suffering from hunger, and incredibly, he was waiting for me to cook and feed them. Combined events pushed me over the edge cerebrally, and I decided right then and there that I would not tolerate it anymore. For the first time, even though he did it many times, I asked him why he didn't feed the kids. Like a rabid animal, the disease did not go away, and I saw the same deep, dark anger on his face. The diseased-behavior was repeated many times before, with the main difference now being that he couldn't hit me anymore.

He said, "I am waiting for you to come and cook as I didn't have a chance."

All of a sudden, I felt a rush of strength and power in me, and I wasn't afraid of Birju anymore. Immediately, I went and started packing our clothes and some of the other necessities. He ran after me, trying to stop me, and begging me to stay, but for the first time, I did not return. Quickly, I went to my kids and explained that we were going to their grandparents' place, and we left once and for all. In the heat of the moment, there was no thinking twice about leaving Birju and my house. But then, when stopping to think about reality, the worry set in as to how I was going to manage on my own. How would I be able to survive as a single parent? Would I be able to give my children the house and yard to play in like they previously had? Instinctively, I knew it would be a difficult but abuse-free journey, and that fact preceded everything else. I was unstoppable at this point.

──── GOLDEN NUGGET ────

Be true to yourself, stand your ground, and never let anyone determine your destiny. It is your journey of life, not anyone else's. In the end, it is you who will have to justify to yourself if the road you chose was what your heart desired. Believe in yourself, and you can achieve anything. Never lose yourself.

CHAPTER FIVE

Live Life with Purpose and Intent

I Act with Bold Courage:
Taking inspiration from the powerful
vision of my future,
I boldly set sail with courage and intent.
I hold my course with focused
attention and relentless commitment,
as I weather the storms of life.

—JONATHAN LOCKWOOD HUIE

For the first time, I developed the strength to fight back, and decided to stand up for myself. It was time for me to follow my heart. After ten years of a less than optimal marriage, I felt as though I had lost myself. I didn't even know how I went from being an independent woman to being so dependent on someone and incapable of doing things I used to do. I was living in a cocoon, and the only way out was to cut through it and escape. Due to many barriers, I knew that it would be a struggle. Getting a divorce was the only option I had, and I knew that it would be an embarrassment for my family.

Moreover, the divorce would result in my family disowning me. I questioned myself many times about whether the divorce was the right decision or not, considering the consequences. My family continued to talk me into compromising and going back to him. I knew that my family would never forgive me for the disgrace the divorce would cause them. Feelings of self-doubt crept in. How was I going to raise my kids as a single mom? How would my kids adapt to all this? Would they blame me for growing up in a broken family? I knew that there would be a long, steep road ahead of me, but I was ready for the challenges. After all, life itself is a daring adventure. If you have not experienced the difficulties of life, then you have not lived.

Think like a queen. A queen is not afraid to fail.
Failure is another stepping stone to greatness.

—OPRAH

Time revealed the difference between a home and a house. I had a different feeling at my parents' home than being in my own house. Unlike my house, my parents' place was a small two-bedroom basement suite they were renting. My parents sold their old home after my dad ended up with a cardiac problem and was unable to continue working. Their home was much smaller than mine, but was warm, welcoming, and peaceful. It was then I realized that it was the peace and comfort inside you that mattered in life, not the worldly things. It is true when people say that "all that glitters is not gold." Owning a beautiful house with numerous amenities is one thing, but being happy is quite another.

Was I happy? The answer is no. Every day I dreaded going back home after work. It was funny that I was scared to go back to my own house. The lone driving factor that made me go home was my children. Life has taught me that home should be where your heart is and something that gives you a sense of belonging. From a psychological perspective, a sense of belonging is a basic human need. It is as essential as food, water, and shelter. Having a feeling of being welcome and connected gives us happiness, and rejection gives us sadness. It's funny how I had put so much effort and money into my dream house, but yet the contentment was missing. My parents' house was a home which I missed having.

After spending a few days of getting settled in my parents' house, I went to the bank to withdraw some money for food and gas from the joint account we had. I remember clearly how hurtful it was when the teller told me that Birju withdrew every penny, and there was no money left in the bank. Is money all that matters in life? What about relationships and family members' safety and well-being? Maybe this is the reason I get personal satisfaction when giving more than receiving? Experience has taught me to do things on my own when feasible and to minimally expect anything from anyone because of expectations, which when unfulfilled, hurt. Likewise, it is essential not to make promises which one cannot keep.

The night before attempting to withdraw funds from the bank, I had promised my kids that I would take them shopping to buy them something, as I knew deep inside that they were missing their big house with all the fancy amenities. Shock could describe that moment. How could someone you gave up everything for and spent almost ten years with be capable of something like this? Birju was hurt and angry at me for leaving him, but what about our children? Some might say, "You decided to leave with your kids, now live with the consequences."

From my perspective, I will never understand that action. One thing I learned from this experience is that you don't know how people will respond until the relationship fails. Realistically, they don't know how you will respond either! Regardless, it's essential to maintain your independence and never lose yourself. After all, you only have one life to live. Do what your heart desires. Accept challenges that life presents, and never doubt yourself. Do the things, within reason, that scare you the most. It is then that you will grow and realize your capabilities. There is always a sunrise after a sunset. It is usually the fear of failure in us that creates the roadblock. We have to overcome the fear in us before we can remove the barriers.

> *When one door closes, another opens, but we often look so long and so regretfully upon the closed door that we do not see the one which has opened for us.*
>
> —ALEXANDER GRAHAM BELL

Admittedly so, that day left me feeling very hurt and helpless. My stomach felt empty. I felt strange when I looked at my kids who were waiting for me to take them to McDonalds and shopping, and who were unaware of my financial crisis. One thing I knew is that I never wanted to be in that situation ever again. On that day, I promised myself that I would do everything in my power to provide my children with everything they deserved. And that particular mentality and goal became my strength. My parents offered assistance until my financial situation improved. Since I graduated from high school, I have always been very independent and felt terrible that my parents had to assist me, especially when they were nearing retirement age. It was a blessing as I don't know what I would have done if they hadn't been there. My parents took us all out for lunch and shopping that day. They bought my son Erin a battery-operated car and my daughter Moni a Barbie doll. That car became my son's favorite toy, and he played with it for many years, and my daughter Moni got into Barbie dolls at that time, starting her collection.

Initially, when I left my house, it was only with what I could carry at the time. So, it was time to go back and get the rest of our things. At that moment, I noticed the key to my house was missing from the key rack. When I asked my parents for the keys, they said, "Birju came and got the key because he lost his." Frustrated, I called Birju to make arrangements to pick up the rest of our stuff. To my surprise, he told me that I would have to go to an attorney to get an order to pick up our stuff. Life is strange in that sometimes you have to get permission from someone else to get your things, which you have worked hard to obtain. It was my fault giving the power to control my life to someone else. From that time on, I have learned that you should never give that power to anyone else. Always be the driver of your own journey. After all, it's your journey, not anyone else's.

*If you feel lost, disappointed, hesitant, or weak,
return to yourself, to who you are, here and
now, and when you get there, you will discover
yourself, like a lotus flower in full bloom, even in
muddy pond, beautiful and strong.*

—Masaru Emoto

Divorce was not easy, but all the challenges just made me stronger. With help from my parents, I hired an attorney and filed for divorce. Shortly after that, I was able to get my things out of my house, even though it took multiple attempts. We agreed the kids would have primary residence with me, and Birju would have alternate weekend visitation. After much wrangling and effort, we procured a legal separation.

The separation was a new chapter of new struggles. It was a struggle to juggle dropping off and picking up the kids. There were times I had to involve my attorney to get the kids back. Finally, I was able to find another part-time job, allowing me to be more financially stable. Birju was unemployed and living off the rental income from the two basements suites from the house, so there was no chance of getting any child support. Regardless of the presence or absence of help from Birju, I was determined to raise my children and give them the life they deserved. Looking back now, some of the turbulence in my life was because I allowed it. Could I have avoided it? I don't have the answer. But definitely, those experiences have taught me many things in life. If anything happens more than twice, there's a good chance of it repeating. For example, the physical and mental abuse in my marriage happened because I accepted and allowed it. Life has taught me that people are who they are. They may change temporarily, but if the circumstances in which they find themselves remain the same, then their response to that circumstance will likely stay the same.

Love yourself enough to set boundaries. Your
time and energy are precious. You get to choose
how you use it. You teach people how to treat you
by deciding what you will and won't accept.

—ANNA TAYLOR

Months passed and the struggles continued. The turbulence in my life continued. My entire experience encompassed two jobs and supporting my two children. Was there more to life than this? At work, I heard stories from my colleagues about their vacation adventures and the fun times with their significant others. Would there be a time in my life when I'd experience a loving relationship? All these were just thoughts until one day, I met someone who made me feel special. We both worked in the same organization. For the first time, I felt something I never felt for anyone before; that burning desire for someone, the instant physical attraction between two people, and the craving to get a glance at that person. There was some unknown force pulling me toward him. Could this be the love I had never experienced in life before? There was some magical feeling when I was around him.

We only flirted with each other since I was still legally married, which placed barriers and boundaries on my end. Why was I so reluctant? Buried under the cultural burden, even in my late twenties, I was still reluctant to do what my heart desired. Fearing what people would say about me dating while yet married. All these thoughts prevented me from moving forward. I knew inside that I wanted to give my all to him, and I knew that there would never be a question of reconciliation of my marriage to Birju. Divorce was imminent; it was just a matter of time. Getting a divorce in Vancouver, Canada at that time was a lengthy process if either party disputed, which he did. It took three years and cost me fifteen thousand dollars to get the divorce finalized. It took three years to sell the house, distribute the funds, and settle the divorce. Several factors elongated the settlement, mainly revolving around Birju not wanting the divorce.

Soon after settlement, I was able to buy a house of my own. It was smaller, but my children were able to have a yard to play in and individual bedrooms. It was a two-level house that gave enough space for my parents to move in with me. They helped me with childcare while I worked two jobs.

Again, it was a blessing that my parents assisted me during my lowest point in life; otherwise, things could have been different for me today. I truly believe that things fall apart because there is something better waiting for us.

Going back to love and romance, you must be wondering what happened to the man who ignited a spark in my life. Did I end up pursuing him or not? The answer is yes, despite being buried under the cultural burden of not dating while still not legally divorced, it was something I had no control over. Maybe it was my mistake and I shouldn't have pursued him, but it seemed right at that time, and I am glad that I did. Indeed, it allowed me to experience a mutually loving relationship. It was a feeling I had never experienced with any man before. Sadly enough, after ten years of a miserable marriage, I still did not know what it felt like to be loved and to love someone in return. It all started when I was swimming through the turbulent waters of my life. Life is always full of surprises. We don't know what life has ahead of us. For the longest time, we just continued talking and flirting with each other like teenagers falling in love for the first time. One day, finally, he came up to me and asked me to meet for coffee after work, and some kind of force prevented me from declining the invitation. We met at a local coffee shop and talked for a long time. We just had so much to share and it felt natural. Why was I so comfortable with this person? Was this how love felt? Life indeed is beautiful when someone makes you feel so special. When it was time for us to go back home, we both stood up, and he quickly grabbed my coat and helped me put it on. Reluctantly, I let him help me with my jacket. He offered to walk me to my car. As I was getting in my car, I looked at him, and he pulled me toward him and whispered in my ear, "Vinnu, I'd like to see you again."

My knees felt weak as I looked into his deep, dark eyes. He slowly moved closer to me, and suddenly, I felt his warm breath, and our lips met. He started kissing me passionately, and I did not want it to stop. Finally, I felt a passion and longing I had never previously experienced. One thing I still remember is that I did not have any control over myself when I was around him.

Many thoughts came to mind that night. Why was I falling for him? Why didn't I feel the same with my husband, who I was married to, and with whom I had two kids? One thing I started to understand for sure was that loving someone and being in love with someone were two different things. When you love someone, you care about that person and want the best for them, but when you are in love with someone, you want to be with that person. There is an intense feeling that you want to spend every minute with that person. Every day, every minute you spend together feels brand new. His whispering softly in my ear about how beautiful I was kept me awake all night and longing to see him again. Birju had always degraded me by saying how ugly I was and how my teeth were so crooked that no one would ever want me if I ever left him. Months passed by, and we continued seeing each other, meeting for coffee, lunch, dinner, walks in the park, movies, etc. I still remember that one foggy evening we were sitting drinking coffee and listening to romantic music. It was that particular evening when my life changed forever. It was Birju's weekend with the children, which gave me the flexibility to be away from home longer. As we were sitting in the car holding each other and watching the sunset by the beach, we started kissing and touching each other. The warmth of his body, passionate kisses, and touch was irresistible. We could feel each other's heartbeats getting faster and faster. One thing led to another, and we decided to spend the night together. It was then I realized what it feels like to love and to be loved. It was a deep intimacy and emotion I had never experienced before. Finally, I realized what really being in love felt like. It was more than just physical enjoyment; it was the connection we had.

Our strong connection and love for each other was apparent by the ways we expressed love for each other. We missed each other terribly when we were not together. There were times that we would drive miles to see each other despite the circumstances. We shared long, passionate kisses under the moonlight. We played in the park under blossoming cherry trees in the spring. We spent hours laying in the park, caressing and holding each other. There was not a time when we got tired of spending time with each other. In summer, when the weather permitted, we walked on the beach, holding hands or just watching the sunset. There were romantic candlelight dinners and surprise flowers to cheer me up or to say how much he loved me.

The best kind of love is the kind which awakens the soul and makes us reach for more, that plants the fire in our hearts and brings peace to our mind.

—NICHOLAS SPARKS,
from *The Notebook*

Two years of being with him was terrific. It gave me the strength to deal with the turbulence in my life. He was not just my lover but also my best friend, always there when needed and never tired of listening to me. After two years, every time we met was like it was our first date. That longing and passion for each other never got old; the spark remained the same as it had been on the very first date. Every love song I listened to was made for us. However, good things sometimes don't last for very long. We had made plans to go to a movie one evening, and he never showed up or called me. Worried, I called him several times, but it went to his voicemail. I did not hear back from him for a few days, and all of a sudden, I received a call. He stated, "I am so sorry, Vinnu, for not going to the movies with you. I had a family emergency I had to take care of."

Being oblivious to the facts, I accepted and believed him and felt sorry for him. It is also true that you cannot hide the truth. No matter how long it takes, one day, it surfaces. I still remember that day we were talking; he told me how he had a great time with his friends the day we were supposed to go to the movie, not remembering what excuse he had given me for letting me down by not showing up. I could not believe what I heard. My heart sank with disappointment. Did he even realize how worried I was? Did he even think how hurtful it was and how much I cried that day? I felt betrayed. It was then he told me how much he loved me and how he couldn't bear losing me. He did it because he felt obligated to his friends. What about the obligation to me? My dad had always taught me to be honest. I was not angry because he chose to spend time with his friends instead of me but because he lied to me. He broke the trust we had. Could I trust him again? How many more things did he lie about that I didn't know? Sometimes it takes years to build trust and just a second to lose. It was tough, but I decided to break up with him despite how much we meant to each other. He spent months begging for forgiveness and bringing me roses, but I stood my ground. He even gave up many things in life to win me back, but my pride and ego prevented me from accepting his apology. Sometimes I do still wonder what my life would have been like if I had forgiven him and stayed with him. We never contacted or saw each other again after the breakup, but the beautiful memories I had with him continue to live within me.

One thing I must say that I have learned from this experience is that honesty and integrity are the fundamentals of a lasting relationship, but we must think and evaluate each situation before jumping to a conclusion. In our journey of life, we meet many people, some are like a shining star and make life worthwhile, and some teach us a lesson. Learn to forgive people. Don't be afraid to apologize. Don't let your pride or ego get in your way. Harvey made a difference in my life by genuinely loving me, which I did not value at the time but realized later in life. In the end, life is all about learning from your mistakes.

At the end, we only regret the chances we didn't take, the relationships we were afraid to have, and decisions we waited too long to make.

—UNKNOWN

It is also true that love comes to us in so many different forms. For some, it is just a physical attraction. For others, it is a spiritual connection that goes beyond physical attraction.

A few years ago, I met a man named Tom. We met through an online dating service. There wasn't any flirting before going on our first date. We mutually liked each other's online pictures and profiles, and started messaging each other. After a few messages, Tom asked me to meet him for dinner at one of his favorite restaurants. It felt kind of strange as we had just started messaging on the same day, but then I thought, *well, there is nothing wrong with having dinner with someone.* If nothing else, I wouldn't have to have another dinner at home, alone. He appeared to have a good sense of humor, which made me not just more comfortable but kind of laugh. As I was driving toward the restaurant, he messaged me, stating which table he was sitting at. Moreover, he told me that he was the guy with a bandage on his nose. What in the world was I getting into?

As I pulled into the parking lot, something urged me to send a message to make sure he was there. Very respectfully, he came and greeted me and took me to the table. My curiosity about the bandage increased since there was no bandage on his nose. Maybe it was my constant staring that made him point to the small transparent dressing on his nose. We still sometimes laugh about it. Everything felt natural at dinner, and we instantly felt a connection. Despite our different beliefs and faith, we decided to date.

We instantly felt comfortable together. Neither of us had to think twice about seeing each other again. As we continued to date, we found our similarities and differences, but the best part was that we were able to resolve things through communication. My relationship with Tom was different from any other relationship I'd had before. There were apparent differences between us, me being Indo-Fijian and him being American. We did have our fair share of disagreements, but we balanced it well. We were reasonable and respectful in the relationship by sharing all the costs fifty-fifty, whether for a simple breakfast, lunch, dinner, or vacation. He often said that he sincerely appreciated me not depending on him, and that I demonstrated a refreshing responsibility in our relationship. This way, we never felt like either of us was taking advantage of the other. In my relationship with Tom, I learned that every relationship tends to be different in its own right. Sometimes it's best not to compare, simply because every relationship is genuinely different. We enjoyed cooking, gardening, sailing in his nineteen-foot sailboat, scuba diving, swimming, snuggling, watching movies, and working on projects together.

One day, out of frustration, I brought up the topic of lack of passion and intimacy in our relationship. Why was my relationship with Tom so different than with Harvey? He then explained to me that his love for me was not only a physical attraction but, more importantly, a spiritual and unconditional *agápē* love.

There must be a stronger foundation than mere friendship or sexual attraction. Unconditional love, agape love, will not be swayed by time or circumstances.

—Stephen Kendrick

Our relationship for the first few months was amazing, without any disagreements. It was like we were on cloud nine. He told me, one night after a party we both attended, that he loved me. We both expressed our love for each other.

Our relationship started to stumble when one day he told me that one of his former employees, a young, single mom named Amy, was coming to stay at his place for few days to train his current employees. I must confess that I was very upset with and told him that it was inappropriate for him to have a female stay at his house alone when he was in a relationship with me.

He laughed and replied, "Babe I don't need your approval to have anyone at my place. I have also known her way before you."

Those words from Tom were very hurtful, but there was lots of truth to what he said. It was his place indeed, and I did not have any right to question him. From my end, I did not want him to seek my approval in any way, but felt it was inappropriate for him to have a female stay with him at his place when we were in a committed relationship. After that event, my outlook on our relationship changed. I didn't feel that there was a necessity to discuss any of our life events with each other anymore. It released us from any obligation of seeking each other's opinion on things. Since then, I have travelled and done things alone or with my friends. This incident with Tom taught me that we should always follow our hearts and do what we desire. We should never justify to anyone what our heart desires. It is, again, our journey of life. When you love someone, you have to let that person be who they are, otherwise you are truly in love with your own image. We should always evaluate our words before we speak, as to how it will impact the other person. You can change your behavior but you can never take back what you've said.

Following your desires, not desires of others.
Doing what you love to do will bring you true
fulfillment in life.

—WANDA VIRGO

Tom acknowledged my frustration and invited me to stay at his condo for the duration of the time Amy was staying. I declined as I did not want him to feel that I did not trust him. In reality, you can't love someone without trust. I took him at his word when he told me that their relationship was purely platonic. I accepted the fact that his business was struggling and he had to get some help. That weekend was Super Bowl weekend as well. Tom organized a small Super Bowl party at his place that weekend. He and Amy prepared everything for the party and invited me over for a few drinks and to watch the game. He also suggested that I spend the night at his place as he did not want me to drive after having a few drinks. Like always, I was excited to spend time with him. We all had some wine and beer.

It was around eleven-thirty at night when he came to me and said, "Babe, you need to go home as I want to discuss business with Amy."

I was confused and shocked at the same time by his request. He had never asked me to leave before. He was always excited to have me at his place. Tom's actions that night hurt me deeply. It was very humiliating to me as I had never been kicked out of anyone's house before. Without saying a word, I packed my things and left his house with tears rolling down my cheeks. Driving back, many things came to my mind: why are people we love and care for the most the ones who hurt us the most? Is it my karma getting back at me for what I did to Harvey? I hurt Harvey deeply although he loved me to a point that he sacrificed everything to prove his love for me. And here, I got kicked out of the house by Tom at night because he wanted to save his business. After a few days, Tom dropped off Amy at the airport and came to my house in the evening to discuss the issue. I was hurt and furious at him for disrespecting and humiliating me in front of Amy.

In his defense, he stated, "Babe, I had no choice as my business is struggling, and I had to discuss the strategies with Amy as to how to turn things around in the office. There is nothing to worry about; it's just a platonic relationship between her and me."

Life is so ironic. I never forgave Harvey, who sacrificed everything to prove his love for me, even his business, but I forgave Tom, who hurt me deeply and humiliated me by kicking me out of his place in the middle of the night so that he could save his business. Despite the anger and disappointment I had toward Tom, I gave our relationship another chance, not because I was desperate or had low self-esteem, but because I had learned to forgive people in life. I had accepted the fact that no one is perfect. Why would I expect perfection from others when I am not perfect myself? As time passed, we learned to communicate better and resolve any differences we had right away, and we tried to make each other a priority. Every person and situation in life teaches us something. Never make decisions in life that leave you with regrets. Never be afraid to apologize. Let go of your ego and pride, and forgive people. I have realized in life that no materialistic things can ever replace loved ones. Never ever say or do things to hurt anyone, as people may forget what you say or do, but never forget how you made them feel.

> *There is no love without forgiveness, and there is no forgiveness without love.*
>
> —BRYANT H. MCGILL

Despite all the issues, there was some kind of connection that kept us together. Tom became more of a friend to me than a lover. He continued to help me and empower me in many areas of my life. Since Tom was a great swimmer and diver, I was envious of his ability to do that, as growing up in Fiji, I never learned to swim. Being underwater was my biggest fear. I tried taking swimming lessons a few times when I was a teenager, but my fear of deep water always got in the way. It seems odd to spend so much time on an island in the South Pacific and have a fear of being in deep water. Tom, at times, laughed at me and made fun of me being an island girl and fearing deep water.

Tom was determined to help me overcome my fear by helping me learn to swim. It was my birthday, and he took me to the local dive shop. At first, I thought he was getting something for himself, but then he asked me to choose fins, a mask, and a snorkel. I must say, that inside me, I was thinking, *why would someone buy me all these as my birthday present when I don't even know how to swim*? Well, Tom had a plan! He was determined to help me overcome my fear of deep water. With Tom's help, I started to slowly learn different swimming strokes in his community pool. I felt like I would drown at first, but after a few tries, I could not even believe that I was capable of floating in the deep end of the pool and able to do laps without any fear. After learning how to swim, Tom encouraged me to take a scuba lesson. I was reluctant at first, but thought it would be a great sport to do it together. I took the course and got certified as an open water and advanced diver. These newfound abilities allowed me to overcome my biggest fear and experience a new world, underwater. I have learned from this experience that you must do the thing you fear the most in life; that is when you will grow and realize your abilities. Since then, I have been to Bonaire, the Caribbean, on a dive excursion, and I also returned to Fiji on vacation and did a shark dive, and soft and hard coral reef dives.

> *You gain strength, courage and confidence by every experience in which you really stop to look fear in the face. You are able to say to yourself, 'I have lived through this horror. I can take the next thing that comes along.' You must do the thing you think you cannot do.*
>
> —ELEANOR ROOSEVELT

Some relationships develop instantly and some over time. In any relationship, respect, trust, honesty, and perseverance is fundamental! Every relationship has different experiences to offer. I am fortunate that life gave me the opportunity to experience both kinds of love in my life. I have learned not to jump on impulse, but to thoroughly evaluate every situation before taking action. Never be a victim of your emotions. Practice self-control; that's where your strength and power is. No relationship is ever a waste. Good relationships teach us what we should accept and bad relationships teach us what not to accept. Things don't always work out the way we want. Never lose hope. Good things usually come when you least expect.

GOLDEN NUGGET

Live your life with intent and purpose. Enjoy little things in life. Cherish special moments, as you don't know if you will have another chance. Appreciate and accept people for who they are and learn to forgive. Make forgiveness a commitment in life instead of an option. Evaluate your words as what kind of impact it will have on others before saying.

CHAPTER SIX

Be a Visionary Person

Our goals can only be reached through a vehicle
of a plan, in which we must fervently believe,
and upon which we must vigorously act.
There is no other route to success.

—PABLO PICASSO

After struggling with divorce for three years, it finally came to an end. My divorce was finalized. The judge granted the divorce despite Birju being out of country, as it had dragged on for three years due to him constantly leaving the country to avoid attending the divorce hearing. It was time for me to close that chapter and move on with my life. My goal now was to reset the sail and start sailing toward the destiny I desired. Creating the life you want is not always easy, as you come across many barriers, but you must have the strength and desire to overcome those barriers to reach that goal. Failures in the journey of our lives are necessary to help us grow and become stronger than before. It is just another step closer to reaching our destiny.

Your goals are the roadmaps that guide you and show you what is possible for your life.

—LES BROWN

After working for ten years as a licensed practical nurse, I decided to further my education and advance my career. As I mentioned, there are many barriers to accomplishing goals, but perseverance is the key to achieving your desired goals. Being a visionary and goal-oriented person, I wanted to get further in life. One day out of curiosity, I decided to go to college and inquire about the general nursing program. To my disappointment, I did not meet the eligibility criteria. There were many requirements I did not have. It was not only disappointing but very discouraging as advanced algebra was one of the prerequisites, which was my weakest subject. Many questions started invading my mind. Would I ever be able to accomplish my goal? Would I be able to get over the barriers to achieving my goal? I cried for days, and then came the fear of being a failure, unable to reach my destiny. Something inside me said, "Vinnu put your heart to it, and you can do it."

I followed my gut instinct and challenged myself. I spent the next few weeks researching colleges, cost, and required courses for the nursing program.

Sometimes you have to get out of your comfort zone and make sacrifices to get what you desire in life. Creating a plan and then executing it was another critical step for me. My project included income versus expenses, time with children, and striking a balance between school and work. There were lots of things to consider; mortgage to pay, raising two children, elderly parents living with me, and working the night shift. There are some things in life you don't have control over. I spent the next three years balancing life with work, school, and home. One thing I must say is that it was challenging, but it gave me a purpose in life, and sometimes that is what you need to remove the roadblocks and enable you to reach your goal.

Don't wait for the storms of your life to pass.
Learn to dance in the rain.

—STEVE RIZZO

Luckily, I was able to find a part-time job to supplement my income and to help with tuition and household expenses. I was finally able to enroll in the required classes for the general nursing program. The first few classes in college went well until I started my algebra class. In my opinion, I did prepare myself well for the course. Unfortunately, I dropped out of math class in tenth grade due to poor performance. As a result, I forgot most of the subject content. As I mentioned before, the key to success is perseverance and believing in yourself. My dream to accomplish my goal was much higher than the fear of failing. I knew that there would be times I would encounter roadblocks, and I would have to remove them in order to reach my destination. My determination and attitude helped.

Fear does not regularly express from my DNA. Enrolling in algebra was addressing and conquering my fear. Fractions and decimals were like Greek to me. Frequent library visits to read and learn math became part of my life. The day finally came when I was confident enough in my abilities and knowledge to enroll in the algebra class. My struggle in the class discouraged me initially, but conquering the course empowered me eventually. Every day I studied like crazy and still failed the tests.

Frustrated, I went to my algebra teacher and said to him, "Sir, I work so hard studying every day, do all my homework, and still I am struggling. What am I doing wrong?"

He answered, "Vinnu, you cannot memorize this subject. You have to understand the content and the rules."

That one suggestion from my teacher changed the way I looked at things in general. Sometimes you have to look at things from a different perspective. There is always a reason why things don't work out in life. Instead of giving up, we need to be analytical and try to understand. By understanding, we develop strategies to make changes to fix things. My way of studying changed from just trying to memorize the math formula to looking deeper and understanding how to solve the problem.

Following my teacher's advice, I aced the final exam and got a personal call of congratulations! That was the only time, in many years of college, I received a personal telephone call from a teacher after an exam. It changed my life for the better. After receiving the news, I broke down in tears of joy and relief all at the same time. This accomplishment set the stage for my enrollment in the nursing program. This small step was a giant leap, getting me closer to my goal of elevating from a licensed practical nurse (LPN) to a registered nurse (RN). Just like the math challenge, we should also try to understand the resistances in our way and to solve the x factor. To this day, this is the formula I follow to address the challenges and resistances in my life.

If you are unable to understand the cause of the problem, it is impossible to solve it.

—Naoto Kan

Passing the algebra course not only gave me hope to succeed in my goals but increased my confidence and self-esteem. Indeed, it was a revelation that anything in life is achievable if you believe in yourself and put your heart in it. After that, I successfully enrolled in the registered nursing program at the University of Victoria. Deep down, it was apparent that the nursing program would require lots of grit and determination. Life at that time required a focused ball of energy, divided among school, work, parents, and my children. Juggling responsibilities became my modus operandi in life. Although there were times I missed Harvey's tender touch, kisses, and good times, I kept myself busy. Life was made easier with very supportive friends I met at work and college.

Indeed, we do not meet people by accident; they always have a role in the journey of our life. Like a diesel train chugging up the mountain, I became lonely for companionship. For many different reasons, I moved on from Harvey. Breaking up with Harvey was very difficult, and it shattered my life and left me with uncertainties in evaluating relationships. One day, I went to my friend's house, feeling down and depressed. She suggested that I start dating for fun, mostly to get over Harvey. At first, there was instinctual resistance to getting involved in another relationship. My friend, tired of watching me mope around, was quite persistent in me getting over myself. She set me up on my first and only blind date with a man who was getting out of a relationship. Although maybe this was not the best plan, at least it was something different. His name was Aden, and we met at a local restaurant by the beach. Aden was also Indo-Fijian, average height, fair-skinned, and had brown eyes. In other words, a very attractive man. It was summer, so the weather was beautiful enough for us to go for a short walk on the beach. We had a great time and ended up continuing to see each other. Aden worked in a manufacturing plant, and I worked as a licensed practical nurse. We continued to see each other almost daily. My first two children, Erin and Moni, got along wonderfully well with Aden. We shared lots of things in common.

Additionally, my parents liked him as well, which was a plus. Aden was more on the quiet side, being introverted. Sometimes when you are a driven and focused woman, others around you instinctively fall behind. Aden was, in a relative sense, more passive. He was a sweet, charming, handsome, outdoorsy man with a good heart. More importantly, he did not physically traumatize me. Aden tended to live for today without an eye for tomorrow, which stood in direct contrast with my goals. For example, there were numerous times when he would spend money on his hobbies without realizing the need for money to run the household with kids and elderly parents. The short story is: I was driven and focused, and he was happy-go-lucky. Some tendencies are more natural to overlook when you are dating.

When getting married and living together, it is another ball of wax. Not realizing this at the time, we ended up getting married. The wedding was in Surrey, BC. After the wedding, we had a week-long honeymoon in Puerto Vallarta, Mexico. We had a great time in Mexico. Since Aden did not have any kids, he wanted to have kids of his own. After getting back from our honeymoon, we decided to start a second family. Shortly afterwards, Aden and I had our first child, a boy we named Nish. Another bundle of joy, beautiful, with lots of thick dark hair. Nish was only six months old when I became pregnant with Aden's second child and my fourth child, named Mani. Mani was beautiful, with light skin, brown hair, and brown eyes just like Aden's. I often think about how blessed I am to have four beautiful children.

Life was getting harder with four children, two from my previous marriage and two from my current marriage. My parents lived with us, and they helped us look after the kids. It was challenging to manage the house while raising four kids with only two incomes. Working two jobs and going to school didn't leave me much time to spend at home. There were goals to accomplish and dreams to fulfill. We tried to spend as much time together as a family as we could, going on camping, boating, and fishing trips. Aden was a good husband and a good father to all our kids but lacked in taking responsibility. I must say that he believed in living his life to the fullest every day. I remember clearly the first time we all went camping in Victoria, BC. None of us knew how to set the tent up. We took the ferry to the island and started driving toward the campground. It was around six o'clock in the evening when we reached the campground. Our campsite was on top of the mountain, with a creek directly behind the tent.

Erin and Moni were excited and eager to learn to set the tent up for the first time. We all got together as a team, and it didn't take much time to set the tent up. It was priceless to see the kids trying to figure out how to set up the tent.

Aden and I started the camping stove and cooked dinner. Our campground was in a no-fire zone, so we missed having a campfire and making s'mores. The next morning, we made breakfast, and Erin and Moni went fishing with Aden. While they were catching fish, I cleaned up the dishes. While sitting outside enjoying the scenery, I heard the kids running toward me, yelling, "Mom, look, I caught a fish."

The look on their faces was priceless. It was a good sized rainbow trout. That evening, we cooked the fish that the kids caught, along with other things we brought. We enjoyed doing the little things together as a family. Life was good, even though we did not have much. Looking back, I realize how precious those moments were. It's the simple things which really matter in life. No amount of money can ever replace the joy of spending time with loved ones.

> *It's the most simple and smallest things in life*
> *that make you realize what true happiness is and*
> *what matters.*
>
> —ABHISHEK TIWARI

The good times, unfortunately, don't always last. Sometimes you have to make an effort to keep the momentum going. In any relationship, you have to make time for each other. Try to do little things for each other to keep the closeness. Don't drift away so far in the ocean that it becomes impossible to swim back to the shore. Our story was somewhat similar. My responsibilities grew bigger, to include: being in the nursing program, raising four children, keeping the house, and paying the bills. The business of life got in the way, and Aden and I started to drift apart. I graduated from my general nursing program and started working as a registered nurse (RN) from seven in the evening to seven in the morning.

Completed BSN program at University of Victoria, Canada, June 2002

Aden worked during the day and sometimes stayed at work late and worked on fixing boat motors, which was his hobby. There were days we didn't even see each other. The distance between us grew greater and greater, until one day we felt like strangers living under the same roof, sharing responsibilities. It was a strange feeling that I never ever want to go through again. It was almost like a replay of my first marriage, minus the abuse. By now, I had gone through enough in life that I did not want to go back and repeat what I went through with my first marriage: living with someone without love and affection, without passion, and without the feeling of being complete. One may say that I was selfish, which I may have been at that time, chasing my dream and trying to find myself. All I longed for was a loving relationship and a good life for my children.

Ten years from now, make sure you can say that you CHOSE your life, you didn't SETTLE for it.

—MANDY HALE

One of the most challenging things in life sometimes is being able to let go of something or someone. I tended to hold on to anger, guilt, grudges, relationships, and personal possessions. Letting go has never been easy for me. Holding on to negative, destructive emotions and relationships can destroy inner peace and can hold one hostage from moving forward. Only when we take responsibility for our personal decisions in life can we achieve freedom from negative emotions and choices in relationships. Every failure in life brings us closer to our success. Instead of blaming ourselves for things we failed to do or didn't do right, we must learn to acknowledge our efforts in life and give ourselves credit. We must learn and grow. Sometimes you have to move on in life to find your own self.

You must make a decision that you are going to move on. It won't happen automatically. You will have to rise up and say: I don't care how hard it is, I don't care how disappointed I am, I am not going to let this get the best of me, I am moving on with my life.

—JOEL OSTEEN

Aden and I realized our differences and decided that it was best to find our own ways in life. He did try to reconcile many times, but I did not want to go back to what I had left. We decided to remain friends and up until now we continue to be good friends. He visits the kids and me anytime we are in Vancouver and even offers to take us places if we don't have means to get around. We don't hold grudges or have any kind of animosity against each other. He is not wealthy enough to support his children financially but is always there for them. We continue to remain good friends.

GOLDEN NUGGET

Don't let your responsibilities get in your way of relationship. Embrace the time spent with loved ones. Make time for your loved ones. Live simply and enjoy little things in life. Don't take things for granted in life.

CHAPTER SEVEN

Moving Forward in Life

In the process of letting go,
You will lose many things from the past,
But will find yourself.

—DEEPAK CHOPRA

After the divorce with Aden, dealing with my relatives became very difficult. The difficulties revolved around cultural and religious expectations and social family embarrassment. Once the divorce with Aden was final, I was now divorced twice. The idea of dating again in my family's eyes was judgmental. Family function invitations were given to me out of a sense of duty, from them to me, and not from a pure desire of wanting me there. Once again, I was standing alone with my four beautiful children. At this point, I could stay in the muck or move on with my life in another area. The choices were a new life or constant bombardment of negativity. Some would say, "It's a great time to get out of Dodge."

While sitting in the break room, one of the nurses on

duty that night started talking about her travel assignment to California. She also mentioned that she was thinking of actually finding a position there and moving permanently. Many thoughts started racing through my mind after listening to her. Her plan immediately resonated in me as it aligned with my internal thoughts about getting out of Dodge. What would it take? What about my children? Would the fathers agree to the relocation? How would it impact the children being away from their fathers? How would I work and still take care of them without the help of my parents?

Timing can be everything. There was a substantial shortage of registered nurses with a bachelor of science degree in nursing at that time in the United States. Quickly, I applied on a job website and got over a hundred offers in different cities in the United States! California was close to Vancouver, and my two brothers, Bob and Yogi, lived in the Los Angeles area. California required a passing score on the National Council of Licensure Exam for Registered Nurses (NCLEX). Although many colleagues discussed with me the profound difficulty in passing that test, it did nothing to deter me from my goal. If anything, it made me more determined to pass that test. Nothing was going to stop me from making a new life for my kids and me.

For the next month, I went into focused overdrive, concentrating on three things in life: kids, work, and studying for the NCLEX test. The defining day came at last, and it was a two-and-a-half hour drive to Seattle, WA. There was an indescribable calm before, during, and after the test. The test generally takes three hours, but I completed it in about one hour! My emotions were a mixture of confidence and concern.

After two weeks of waiting, the letter from the California Nursing Board came in the mail. My heartbeat got faster and faster. Quickly, I opened the letter and, to my surprise and amazement but not against my gut feeling, I had passed the test on the first try! My eyes filled with tears, and I felt nauseated. My life just opened up in front of me like how a butterfly must feel coming out of its cocoon.

When life gives you something that makes you
feel afraid, that's when life gives you the chance
to be brave.

—Lupytha Harmin

It took six months before I was able to get my California Nursing License, get a job offer letter from a hospital in California, and sell my house. My parents had been living with me in exchange for babysitting. My departure meant that they had to move in with my sister. In life, when you make a big move, you give up something to get something else.

The hospital was very accommodating. They found reasonable housing for me, paid my immigration fees, funded the move, and gave me a nice sign-on bonus. We moved to a small town in California, called Visalia. There was a big difference between living in Vancouver, BC, and Visalia, California. Oddly, I've never seen anyone get so excited about a rainstorm. All of the nurses ran outside when it started to rain like it was gold coming down to fill their treasure chests. In Vancouver, it rained five out of seven days in the week. This regular gratitude to the rain Gods made me laugh. The cost of living was much more reasonable in Visalia over coastal areas such as Los Angeles.

Moreover, it was only a two-hour drive to the beach, twenty minutes to the beautiful redwoods in the Sequoia Mountains, and three hours to both of my brothers in Los Angeles. Soon after we got settled in Visalia, my mom stayed with us to help in the transition. It was a blessing to have my mom for many reasons that included: her help with the kids, going for walks, shopping, cooking together, sitting by the pool, getting our nails and hair done, and doing mom and daughter things. In short, there is nothing like a mom in this world!

We lived in a rather tight but cozy two-bedroom apartment for three months to establish a domicile. Shortly after that, I bought a house of our own. It was a small three-bedroom house but was perfect for us. The house was kid-friendly with a pool, jacuzzi, and yard, to include fruit trees and a gazebo. Things finally started to fall into place. My income sources were limited to my pay as a nurse. The deal with my ex-husbands was that I could take the kids out of Dodge, but in exchange, we would not receive child support. The essential thing was peace and contentment. We were finally there! My parents continued to travel back and forth between Vancouver and Visalia to help with the kids. The reality is, I could not have done it without them. The expense increased as the kids got older, which drove me to find a second on-call nursing job at Cochrane Prison, a maximum-security prison. It was interesting, as all my life I was a shy and timid girl. Now I was wearing a shield and going into prisoners' cells with a guard to give them medication. There was no room for second thought as I needed money to make ends meet.

You don't know how strong you are until strong is the only choice you have.

—Bob Marley

The better pay enabled me to get a housekeeper to manage the house and kids when I was at work, which took a great load off my shoulders. Most definitely, I did my best to be their mom and dad, but there were times I felt like a failure. There was one particular Christmas, which has taught me many things in life. Financially, I was struggling but didn't want my children to know that.

My two older kids, Erin and Moni, went to Vancouver to spend Christmas with my parents by themselves since I was unable to get time off. I stayed in California with my two younger kids, Nish and Mani. As was true every year, I wanted them to have expensive presents under the Christmas tree but could not afford this due to financial difficulties. Luckily, I had my old Christmas tree from the previous year, so I did not have to buy one. Secretly, one day, I went to a Dollar Store and bought, wrapped, and placed presents for them under the tree. My kids were as excited about the presents from the Dollar Store as they were from the higher end stores. I missed having Erin and Moni, but I tried to make the most of it with Nish and Mani, even with what little we had. My older kids, Erin and Moni, had a great time in Vancouver with my parents and family. Christmas that year taught me the little things in life are what matter. It was not about expensive presents but family time during the holiday season. At that point, I resolved to keep things real but also not to have to struggle to buy gifts at Christmas. After returning home from Vancouver, Moni and Erin told me that they had no intention of staying in California after their high school graduation. They were missing their friends, grandparents, and sports activities. Erin and Moni went back to live with my parents in Vancouver as they had told me, despite me encouraging them to finish their college while living with me. My parents were happy to have them as they were feeling lonely and missed having them around. It was heartbreaking, but as a parent, I knew that I would have to let them fly. No matter where they lived, my love for them was always there. Although they continued to visit from time to time, now it was just Mani, Nish, and I left in Visalia.

Life continued until one day, I realized that I wasn't getting anywhere in life with my current nursing position, which had no upward room for advancement. Additionally, gangs were taking over, and it was not the best place to raise my kids. Once again, my search for a new job began. As I have mentioned before, everything in life happens for a reason. After a few months of looking, I finally got a job offer from a large academic medical center in Richmond, Virginia. Like the other moves, it was exciting and scary at the same time. The kids were the "rocks" in the relocating.

Moving did not seem to bother them as much as it did to me. Before making any decisions, like my dad, I had a family meeting during dinner to discuss and review the opportunity and how it would positively impact us. To my surprise, instead of getting frustrated and upset, they were excited about the change and eager to make new friends. It took several months before I was even ready to move. Before the move, I was able to sell my house and make a significant profit, which helped me with the move and allowed me to buy a home in Virginia.

The day of the move finally arrived, and we packed our things in the car and started driving from California to Virginia. It was a long drive. We drove during the day, enjoying the scenery and stopping in cities to eat and rest. One of the places we explored was the Grand Canyon. Always wanting to visit there, it made perfect sense to seize the opportunity. We celebrated Thanksgiving in a gas station restaurant. It was one of the best turkey dinners as I did not have to cook it, and we were hungry. It was not our typical Thanksgiving dinner. We missed Erin and Moni as every previous year we had eaten Thanksgiving dinner together and went shopping the next day. All of us missed Erin and Moni, but we made the most of the Thanksgiving dinner that day. Indeed, it is a life lesson to make the most of who you are with and what you have.

Be thankful for what you have; you'll end up having more. If you concentrate on what you don't have, you will never, ever have enough.

—OPRAH WINFREY

After driving for a few days, we finally reached our destination in Richmond, Virginia. Luckily, we moved during the holiday season, so we had at least a month to settle before starting school and work. After a month of staying in an extended stay hotel, we finally moved into our new place. The house was a three-level, 3600 square foot house with vinyl siding, built on a two-acre wooded lot with a creek running in the back. There was a large lake close to our house, called Lake Chesdin. Sometimes we went there to fish or watch turtles.

Christmas that year was quieter than every other year, with just the three of us, but we made the most of it by putting up a fresh-cut, local Christmas tree, decorating the house, and making our traditional turkey dinner. In January, the kids started school, and I started my new job at Virginia Commonwealth University. Luckily, the school bus picked them up and dropped them off in front of the house since the school was about five miles away. It took some of the load off my shoulders since the distance between my work and home was about twenty-five miles, and it would have been impossible to drop them off and pick them up from school. It was a great family-oriented neighborhood where everyone looked out for each other. Nish and Mani made a few friends from the same school and area right away, which was quite helpful.

My new job was fascinating and presented me with many opportunities. It was a large, University-based academic medical center. Three months into my new position, the clinical nurse educator on the unit resigned. My manager urged me to apply for the clinical nurse educator position. A master's degree in nursing was a requirement that I did not have at that time.

Reluctantly, I went to my manager and said, "I don't think I can apply for the position because I don't have my master's degree, and it is one of the requirements."

She looked at me, smiling, and she said, "Don't worry; I have taken care of all that." I was confused. She saw the disappointed and confused look on my face and exclaimed, "We will move you into the position and get you enrolled in the master's program. You will have two years to complete it."

My thought was that this was an excellent opportunity, but I would never be able to do it due to my financial responsibilities. At that point, she told me that since a master's degree was a requirement, the tuition would be taken care of by the organization. Well, it was an opportunity I could not pass up. So, as of April 2007, I took the new leadership position as a clinical nurse educator. Immediately, I started my online program to obtain a Master of Science degree in Nursing. Being in that position, I was able to mentor the students and nurses in the unit. The new status at work changed my outlook on nursing. Just seeing the students and novice nurses accomplishing things they never anticipated gave me personal satisfaction I had never experienced before. It gave meaning to my career. It was not the money that mattered the most but the personal and professional joy of making a difference in someone's life.

When you are inspired by some great purpose, some extraordinary project, all your thoughts break their bounds. Your mind transcends limitations, your consciousness expands in every direction, and you find yourself in a new, great and wonderful world. Dormant forces, faculties and talents become alive and you discover yourself to be a greater person by far than you ever dreamed yourself to be.

—PATANJALI

It was December of 2009 when I finally completed my Master of Science in Nursing degree (MSN). My parents were very excited and proud of me when I told them about it. As it turns out, I was the only one among my siblings to obtain master's degree. The plan was to have a celebration with my parents in Vancouver after the kids' school year ended in May 2010. In April 2010, my mom called and told me that my dad was in the hospital with cellulitis in his right toe. My dad and I talked on the phone almost every day during his hospitalization. He updated me about his test results and his condition. I remember one day, he called me and said that he missed watching his sports channel, which was not viewable on his room televison (TV). Without his knowledge, I called the hospital and added the sports channel to his TV. It was priceless when my dad called me the next day, telling me that he was finally able to watch his favorite sports channel. It's the little things we do in life for people that matter.

It was toward the end of May when my dad suddenly started to decline. He had a stroke and wasn't able to communicate anymore. My mom called me and wanted me to come to Vancouver as my family wanted me to be my dad's healthcare surrogate. It was the beginning of June when I went to Vancouver with my kids to be with my dad. My dad was in one of the hospitals I had worked in before. I had never imagined that I would be taking care of my dad there. All my siblings were there except my brother Nesh as he was unable to get a visa from Fiji. Nish, Mani, and I flew to Vancouver. We met my mom, Erin, Moni, Bob, and Nish at my dad's hospital bed. My dad was very fragile and sick. He smiled at us and held our hands but was unable to say anything.

Tears started to roll from my eyes. That evening, I helped the nurses put my dad to bed and then went home. All night, I kept reflecting on everything he had done for us. He had worked so hard for us in his life. It was nice to have my older brother Bob there. He was very supportive and reassuring.

Early the next morning, I went to the hospital to help my dad with morning care and breakfast. After breakfast, I helped my dad get in a wheelchair and took him to the cafeteria. I read the newspaper and tried to get him to communicate by writing. He tried but was unsuccessful most of the time. My siblings also shared in caring for my dad in order to give each other a break. We rotated duties for a few weeks. One morning, when my brother Bob and I went to help my dad at five-thirty in the morning, I saw tears in my dad's eyes. With my nursing experience, I knew that my dad was about to leave us forever. I told my brother to inform my mom and everyone else to come to the hospital.

My brother Bob, being a Hindu Priest, started saying prayers, and I held my dad's hand while he took his last breath. Slowly, my dad passed away while I was holding his hand. I closed his eyes and informed the staff on the unit. My brother Bob and I sat there, just reflecting on everything until my mom and the rest of the family came. Being a nurse, I had experienced losing my patients, but this was the first time I had experienced losing someone so close to me. It was the pain I couldn't explain. I felt numb, unable to even express the sorrow I was feeling.

Some people come into our lives and quickly go. Some people move our soul to dance. They awaken us to new understanding with passing whisper of their wisdom. Some people make the sky more beautiful to gaze upon. They stay in our lives for a while, leave footprints in our hearts, and we are never, ever the same again.

—FLAVIA WEEDN

It was a very traumatic time for me. I was given the responsibility of arranging the funeral service for my dad and other logistics. There is a saying, "When it rains, it pours." At the funeral service, I distinctly remember a relative coming to me and telling me that my son, Nish, was not feeling well.

I ran to see what was going on and then, all of a sudden, he looked at me and said, "Mom, I can't breathe."

My heart sank as I saw him going down to the floor. Moni, my eldest daughter, immediately started cardiopulmonary resuscitation (CPR) while I called the ambulance. Luckily, the ambulance was there within a few minutes. My son, Nish, went to the hospital in respiratory distress. My dad, at the very same time, was being cremated inside the funeral home. Nish was attended to for a few hours in the emergency room (ER). He got discharged with a diagnosis of an asthma attack.

Concerned about Nish, I booked the earliest flight and returned to Virginia with Nish and Mani. I was still in shock about everything that happened in Vancouver. For the first time, I experienced what we call delayed grief. I was driving to work and all of a sudden, I started crying. My heart felt heavy. All I could think about and picture was my dad's face and the time I spent with him.

Life is not fair sometimes. Upon returning to work, I found out that my manager and colleagues transferred to another unit in the hospital, which changed lots of things at work. Nish also started having lots of additional respiratory problems and had to be admitted to the hospital frequently. The allergist tested him, and found he was allergic to some of the trees indigenous to Virginia and our backyard. Although I loved my job, my son's health was more important to me. It preceded my career. Once again, it was time to seek another job and move.

The following year, in April, I found a great job as a nursing outcomes improvement facilitator in Springfield, Illinois. It was a leadership position with an excellent salary, relocation package, and room for advancement.

Life is like a box of chocolates. You never know what you're gonna get.

—Forrest Gump

Like every other move, Nish, Mani, and I were excited to move to a new place, allowing all of us to meet new people. Most importantly, the hope was that Nish's respiratory issues would resolve. Based on the statistics, Springfield, Illinois had a lower allergy rate than Richmond, Virginia. I accepted the job offer, and we all moved to Springfield, Illinois, in May of 2011. The kids were ecstatic about the extended summer vacation. That gave us extra time to get acquainted with our new home. My job was fascinating and different from my previous nursing roles. The new position had a lot to offer. Fortunately, when completing my Master of Science degree in Nursing, I had completed the capstone project in pain management. Quickly, I became a pain management specialist and performed pain consultations for physicians and trained the nurses to be pain resource champions.

Additionally, my new job requirement was to increase patient satisfaction in pain management for the entire hospital. Through perseverance and hard work, our hospital became a top-level hospital in patient satisfaction. The hospital exceeded its benchmark for the Hospital Consumer Assessment of Healthcare Providers Systems (HCAHPS) pain management survey within six months of my taking that role. Radio stations featured me in their programs, which was exciting for me, my kids, and my friends. My manager was an amazing woman, had excellent leadership skills, was a great mentor, and was very caring and empowering. Through her encouragement and leadership, I was able to drive forward to my goals and accomplishments.

After six months, I bought a four-bedroom, four-bath, three-level house on 1.8 acres, with a pool, hot tub, firepit, and an in-house theater room. We picked a family-oriented neighborhood with many cookouts, parties, and get-togethers. We met some fantastic people who became, and continue to be, my friends.

Life is partly what we make it, and partly what is made by the friends we choose.

—TENNESSEE WILLIAMS

Despite the fun and friends, winters can be cruel in Illinois. Quickly, I realized I did not want to spend the rest of my life in such an environment.

In 2014, I went on a cruise to the Caribbean and, upon return, found out that my manager, with whom I was very close, had decided to retire. The news of her resignation impacted me emotionally. Working with her had been very refreshing and empowering. I was happy for her but sad to see her leave, and I realized that the department would never be the same again in her absence. I would surely miss her and her expertise deeply.

Shortly after her departure, a new position of senior oncology research nurse opened up for me. The new job was much different, but I learned and settled into it very quickly. In that role, I worked with cancer patients who were on a clinical trial. All of these patients had exhausted their treatment options. Short story, they were in dire straits. It was up to me to help find a solution for their continued survival. Amid many patients, one brain cancer patient stood out as special. Both he and his wife were very appreciative of my efforts to help. We met weekly during his chemotherapy infusion for a required assessment.

We became very close. One day, during my regular visit to the clinic, I realized that it was his birthday. I held his hand and said, "Happy birthday. Are you celebrating with your family later?"

He looked at me, smiled, and said, "I am old, sick, and about to die, so no one wants to celebrate with me."

I saw the sadness in his face, as well as his wife's. It broke my heart. After going to the coffee shop and picking up a small birthday cake, we celebrated his birthday in the infusion clinic. The look on his face was priceless. I realized at that moment that no materialistic thing in the world could replace that. Again, it is the little things in life that make a difference. I must say that there was a particular satisfaction in working with the oncology population.

Never stop doing little things for others. Sometimes those little things occupy the biggest part of their heart.

—UNKNOWN

Living in Springfield, Illinois, continued to be a challenge, but we made the most of it by enjoying our beautiful house, friends, and by spending vacations in either Florida or the Caribbean. My passion for Florida kept growing with each vacation. Everything in Florida reminded me of the Fiji Islands. Five years went by quickly, and Nish and Mani graduated from high school. My kids were adults, so it was easier to discuss our relocation to Florida. Fortunately, they were not opposed to making another move.

My children, Nish and Mani, were quiet for a while before Mani finally broke the silence and said, "Mom, you have worked very hard all your life. Now is the time for you to enjoy and do what your heart desires."

My eyes filled with tears. The emotional spectrum ran between terminal points of feeling happy that my kids were supportive and feeling guilty that they would have to leave their friends. We moved to Florida in 2016, and it was a critical time in life for me.

After getting settled in Florida, my life started to fall into place. My dreams started to come true. For instance, I was offered a position as an oncology nurse navigator at a large healthcare system in Ft, Myers, Florida. As a nurse navigator, I guide patients through the care continuum and help address and eliminate any barriers they may have during their cancer journey. This job allowed me to earn a specialty certification in oncology (OCN) as well. With this position, I was able to apply all the talents acquired over the years in one occupational position. The job allowed me to combine my experience and skills with my passion for helping oncology patients. It also afforded me the chance to make a difference in the lives of others without expectation, which enabled me to carry on my dad's legacy.

When I chased after money, I never had enough.
When I got my life on purpose and focused on
giving of myself and everything that arrived in
my life, then I was prosperous.

—Dr. Wayne Dyer

The home I purchased was of perfect size and characteristics, along with a large backyard and tropical plants similar to what I liked in Fiji. In particular, I loved the coconut palms, mango trees, hibiscus flower bush, plumerias, and gardenias. One thing I wanted immensely was an extensive orchid garden. Shortly after moving in, we realized the existing orchid garden was over the property line with our neighbor. We designed and rebuilt a newer, more extensive brand-new orchid garden on my property in less than three weeks! Although it was very stressful to hear that we needed to move the orchid garden off of the neighbor's property, it resulted in a much better orchid garden that also served as an excellent barrier on the edge of my property. Such experiences remind me that growth occurs when we are under pressure in life. Of all the places, I have never felt as content about living anywhere as I do in Florida. Life is indeed what you make it. Sometimes, you have to go through many twists and turns, ups and downs in life to reach your destination. The key is, again, to never give up.

Like other places I have lived, I also made some great connections with people here in Florida. Best of all, my colleagues at work became my work family. A good example of this came during hurricane Irma, a category five hurricane. The area I live in had a mandatory evacuation order due to the danger of storm surge. My best friend Lis, who was my neighbor in Springfield, Illinois, now living in Pensacola, Florida, offered me shelter at her place. Having provided a shelter indeed was a blessing as I waited too long to evacuate, and none of the shelters in Fort Myers were available. Though I was troubled about Hurricane Irma, it was nice to be able to spend a few days with my best friend. We cooked together and drank wine, just like when we were neighbors. Upon returning to my home after a few days post-hurricane, I found that my garden had been destroyed. There was a forty-year-old pony palm tree in front of my house which had been uprooted and missed hitting my house by just a few inches.

I was devastated when I looked at my yard. Everything I loved around the house had been destroyed. All of a sudden, I didn't want to be there anymore. It seemed like my world just crashed right in front of me. My phone rang; it was my supervisor, who is a very caring and compassionate woman, checking on me.

She asked, "Are you home?

I started sobbing, and I replied, "Yes, but everything is gone."

Confused she asked me, "Is the house okay?"

I replied, "Yes, but my garden, which I love, is destroyed."

She comforted me by saying that everything would be okay, and since I still did not have any power, she offered for me to stay at her house. Before the hurricane, I had bought a few battery-operated fans and had a propane grill, so I was okay at my place.

Following the weekend, my work family came to my house with their families and cleaned up my entire yard. One of my colleagues gave me plumeria cuttings to plant in my garden, knowing how much I love plumerias. Being distraught about how I was going to remove the uprooted pony palm from the yard, I posted on the community Facebook page for help. To my surprise, someone from my neighborhood came and removed the giant pony palm from my yard without charging me any money. I had no words to express the appreciation. It was like a miracle. Within a year, my garden looked much better than before. I truly believe God sends people who are human angels to help us when we run out of resources. When you give without expectations, help comes to you without you expecting it. I would never have been able to turn around my yard if it wasn't for my colleagues. I am so blessed and fortunate to have so many caring and considerate people in my life.

—— GOLDEN NUGGET ——

Pursue the occupation, place, and activities your heart desire. Give without expectations. You will get rewarded when you least expect. Never, ever underestimate the difference you can make in someone's life by reaching out and helping.

CHAPTER EIGHT

Recreating My Footprints

*When you finally go back to your old home, you
find it wasn't the old home you missed,
but the childhood.*

—SAM EWING

*Some memories are unforgettable,
remaining ever vivid and heartwarming.*

—JOSEPH B WIRTHLIN

After a long, eleven-hour flight, I finally landed at Nadi International Airport. Curiosity about the place I left a long time ago but was never really able to detach myself from increased. My cousin Devi, who I had not seen for forty-two years, would be meeting me at the airport. We used to go to school together, play together, go to movies together, etc. It seemed like yesterday. I struggled to get myself out of the airplane, longing to feel the fresh island breeze, to see friendly welcoming smiles, to see Devi, my family, and friends, and to revisit the property I used to explore as a little girl. I was desperate to walk on the same road and feel the sand under my bare feet the same way it felt when I was a little girl running downhill from my house to the beach.

Walking toward the baggage claim, I immediately started noticing changes. It looked so different from the picture I had in my mind of the past. Was it my vision about things that had changed, living abroad after such a long time, or had the island gone through changes due to tourism? Would I be disappointed seeing all the changes and not finding some of the things which were still embedded in my memory? I was about to discover that. It felt weird getting a permit to stay for only six months in the place I was born and that was once my home. I saw a small coffee shop in the area of a restaurant where I used to eat with my parents whenever we came to the airport. The picture of the excellent island food was still clear in my memory. Is losing originality needed in life? Why do we have to keep up with the rat race? Now, seeing all the changes not only saddened me but also disappointed me. After being on the plane for such a long time, I was craving a good cup of coffee, and that coffee shop which disappointed me happened to be right in front of me. With the disappointment on my face, I walked into the coffee shop, along with my big suitcases.

The girl at the counter smiled and said, "Good morning ma'am, it looks like you had a long flight. Can I give you our exceptional coffee?

Forcing myself to smile, I said, "Sure, black coffee without sugar."

I noticed how much pride that girl took in preparing that cup of coffee for me to help me with the aftermath of the long journey, and here I was disappointed to see the new coffee shop. Why are we so reluctant to accept change? Why do we get stuck in the past and fail to see the benefit that change brings? Over the years, I have changed in life as well, from drinking tea to drinking coffee, walking barefoot to wearing shoes, living without electricity to having many of the luxuries in life. So, what was I disappointed about, seeing the coffee shop there instead of my favorite restaurant from years ago? Taking a sip from that cup of coffee and realizing how satisfying it was changed my entire attitude, from being disappointed to being grateful that the new coffee shop was there. This experience made me be more accepting of changes and to look at changes in our lives from a different perspective. To be more open and to go with the flow in life instead of being rigid. Why can't we accept changes around us when we go through so many changes? I smiled and thanked her for making my day with a fantastic cup of coffee. It's just little things in life that should matter. That smile, positive approach, and being sensitive to other's needs. While enjoying a great cup of coffee, I suddenly turned around and saw my cousin Devi standing there. I could not believe my eyes; after forty-two long years, she was standing right in front of me. We looked at each other for a while and ran and hugged each other. It seemed like it was just yesterday; we used to walk to school together, laugh together, play together, and watch out for each other. Here we are now living in different parts of the world but still able to reconnect in person again. As we were drinking coffee together, a man waved at us, walked toward us, and addressed my cousin by her name. He said that our rental car was ready. It was time to get on the road. We started our journey to explore the place where we grew up. Our hotel was approximately two hours away. On the way to the hotel, on a narrow road between sugar cane and farm, I started carefully observing everything.

We passed many villages, and local people waving and smiling at us. There were fruit and vegetable stalls in front of the villagers, and children playing with each other. Over years of being away, I forgot how beautiful Fiji was. The greenery, the mountain, the rainforest, the smiles on everyone's faces, and children in uniforms, walking together to school, laughing, and being playful. The villagers didn't have much, but they looked content and stress-free. All the children still played together outside, instead of being homebound, playing video games. Life in villages was like being part of one big, happy family, everyone there for each other—what a beautiful experience. I was starting to get very envious.

We finally arrived at the oceanfront hotel. All the years I have lived in Fiji, I had never stayed in a hotel, as my parents were never able to afford that expense. It was only for the tourists visiting Fiji. I was exhausted from traveling, so I rested the remainder of the day at the hotel, enjoying the amenities it offered. It was tough for me to sleep that night, due to the sixteen-hour time difference. Next morning, we headed out to see my brother and his family in a small town called Cuvu. It is beautifully nestled in Coral Coast. It took us awhile to find my brother Nesh's house. After a long search and asking many people in the neighborhood, we finally were able to find Nesh's home. Since this was my first time visiting his house, I honestly didn't know what to expect. The car finally pulled into a well-maintained yard, and I saw my brother Nesh rush out, followed by his daughter-in-law, my nephew Jay, and grandkids whom I had never met. They welcomed us into the house and prepared coffee for us.

My brother, his family, and I sat and reflected on many things we did when we were kids. Things were so different now. We live thousands of miles away and barely see each other. As kids, we used to play with our cousins, but now we all live in different countries and hardly see each other. Sitting on my brother's porch, feeling the cool breeze sweeping my face, I saw the happiness and excitement on my brother's face. The kids, sitting by me, looking at me, were eager to hear what I had to say. I started to think how important it is in life to stay connected with family. We get so caught up in the rat race in our life that we forget to make time to reconnect with our loved ones. I could have taken time out of my busy schedule to visit my family but I didn't; I could have easily, but I chose not to. Sometimes in life, we tend to value materialistic things more than people. We forget that we can always replace materialistic things but not people. We tend to learn a lot of things during our journey of life, and I finally understood the value of people in my life. It is all about balancing things in life. The next few days were spent visiting my brother Nesh, going to a traditional Fijian market to buy fresh fruits, which I had been craving since I booked my flight, and enjoying the resort life. We watched the traditional Fijian dance called Meke, Kava ceremony, fire dance, and the beating of Lalli drum—an Idiophonic Fijian drum made of wood with a slit in the middle that makes musical sound when beaten with two wooden sticks. It is used as a form of communication. The day finally came to actually go diving and see everything underwater that I used to see from the edge of the reef as a little girl. The difference was that now I would be able to actually experience it underwater. I went to Collosium in Beqa Lagoon to experience the shark feed, and to Pinnacle Reef and DreamWorks Reef to experience the corals. The experience was terrific. The rainbow-colored corals and the colorful fishes were just unbelievable. It was a dream come true experience. Life is strange; little did I know as a child, when admiring the colorful corals and marine life that, in fact, one day, I would be able to experience all that underwater. The night before the dive, I kept tossing and turning, reflecting back on my time as a little girl running to the edge of the reef and admiring everything I saw underwater. In the morning, I took a cab to the dive shop. There, I got changed into my diving outfit and got on the dive boat. It was about a forty-five-minute ride from Coral Coast, Fiji to Beqa Lagoon. It was a bumpy boat ride to the dive location, due to strong winds. The swells were up to approximately six feet high. It took me back down memory lane, when I used to go on boat rides with my dad as a little girl, sitting on the edge of the boat without any fear of falling. Things were different now, due to safety awareness. The thought made me smile. The view of the island from the boat in the ocean was just amazing. I forgot how beautiful the place I was born in looked: the lush mountains, white sandy beaches, and deep blue sea. Thoughts of my dad kept coming back. Life was so peaceful and serene back then.

The boat stopped and the voice of our divemaster saying, "Welcome to Beqa Lagoon," startled me.

Along with the rest of the divers, I put on my dive gear, anxious to see if the beauty of the underwater world I used to see from the surface was the same. One by one, we entered the water. Using a rope, we went down to explore the beauty of the underwater world. The magic of what I had always wondered about was right in front of my eyes as I studied the many different colorful corals and fish.

The next day, I headed toward Dawasamu, Fiji, where I was born. The drive was terrible and very dangerous, with many hills and winding, bumpy gravel roads. I sat on the front passenger seat, holding the car seat tightly, and my cousin Devi did the driving. My brother Nesh was seated at the back, reflecting on and telling us stories of our childhood days. The car finally stopped at a resort called Takalana Bay. We got out of the vehicle, and a middle-aged indigenous man named David greeted us. He welcomed us and asked if we wanted to check into the resort. I walked around, looking at the resort. It was a two-villa resort. Each villa had two bedrooms, a kitchen, a bathroom, and overlooked a view of the ocean. While walking around, I ended up on the balcony overlooking my dad's property. The resort was on what was once my uncle's estate, next to our property. David came and stood beside me, looking at my dad's property with me.

Many thoughts were clouding my brain, and suddenly I turned toward him and said, "I used to live there," pointing at the property.

He jumped with astonishment, looked at me, and asked, "Are you the daughter of the boss?"

I nodded. The villagers used to call my dad "boss," as he owned the farm, store, and rice mill. Many villagers worked on my dad's farm. He looked at me in astonishment and ran to Nesh and Devi, shaking his head in astonishment. My brother asked him about a few villagers he used to hang out with, but sadly they had all passed away. There was one particular girl called Mere whom I wanted to meet. She used to come to my house to pick mangoes from one of our mango trees. My personality was so different when I was little. Despite being an introvert, I was very possessive of things on our property. There were times when I would confront her with a stick and stop her from picking mangoes. Once again, it felt like I was standing there and watching a movie of my childhood.

I turned around and asked David, "Does Mere still live in the village here?"

He answered, "No, unfortunately, she passed away a few years ago."

It was kind of scary that everyone we knew had passed away. Strange thoughts crept through my mind. Would I have passed away too if I had stayed here? Was it because of a lack of resources and lack of a medical facility? Some things I will never know. I asked David if it was okay for us to go see where my house used to be. He said that the house was not there anymore, but the foundation was still there. Everything looked so different now. Our property, where I used to run around as a little girl, seemed so much smaller now. I chose to walk on the same path toward my house as I used to when I lived there. The road still existed as before. After walking for ten minutes, we were standing on the property that was once my dad's and my little paradise. For a long time, I sat on one of the trees that my brother Munna and I used to sit on and catch fish from. It was a dilo tree, and part of it was on top of the water. As I walked toward the tree, I noticed that I was recreating the footprints on the beach, which I loved to walk every morning. It was a fantastic feeling, difficult to express. All of a sudden, I remembered the little stream where Munna and I used to hide the dinghy. We started envisioning everything and tried to connect past to present. Everything was still there, except for the house. The mangrove tree to which we tied the dinghy in the stream was still there. My eyes were full of tears as I started to walk back to the resort. My brother Nesh came and hugged me. We both held each other and cried awhile, before continued to walk on the same path, recreating our footprints.

Beach I used to play as a child, Dawasamu, Fiji Islands.
Picture taken September, 2019.

We finally reached the resort. David's wife, Sara, surprised us by cooking lunch for us. We did not want to impose, but David insisted that we have lunch with them. He said that it would be an honor for us to have lunch with them. Sara was an indigenous Fijian but made both Fijian and Indian dishes. She made curried chicken, eggplant, roast cassava root, and salad. It was nice to relax and enjoy lunch, looking at the view of the ocean.

It was time for us to continue our journey to Suva, the capital city of Fiji, where I had lived after moving from Dawasamu, until I moved to Vancouver. My eyes couldn't believe the changes in Suva. It was so different. There were large malls and fast food joints like McDonald's and Burger King. The car stopped at the Grand Pacific Hotel, which was built in 1916. Many well-known people had stayed there. It was located across from Albert Park, where I used to attend the Hibiscus Festival with my mom, cousins, and grandma. I clearly remember that day I stopped in front of the hotel on the way to the festival, looking at the hotel.

My mom looked at me and asked me why I stopped. Looking at the hotel, I asked my mom, "What is that, Mom, with so many lights?"

My mom said, "That is a very expensive hotel. Only rich and famous can stay. It's not for us."

I was sad and kept walking to the festival with my mom, inside of me longing to see the inside of the hotel one day. Here I was today, checking in at the same hotel. As my brother Nesh and I walked toward our rooms, I kept looking at the interior of the hotel, amazed that all the original things were still preserved, even after the recent renovation. My curiosity to see the room kept increasing, as I heard from my mom that everything was very classy inside. As I opened the door of the room, I saw a large balcony overlooking the park where I used to stand and look at the hotel with my mom. I went straight to the balcony and kept looking at the park. I could almost picture myself standing there with my mom during the festival, looking at the hotel, holding her hand. My eyes filled with tears.

That evening, Nesh and I went wandering in Suva City after eating at the hotel restaurant by the water. It was nighttime when we returned to the hotel. Before going in the hotel, I stood outside and admired the lights, as I used to when I was little. The hotel was glowing at night, exactly the same way as before.

Everything still looked the same, only I wasn't little anymore, and I was there without my mom. I missed her terribly and wished she could have been with me.

Grand Pacific Hotel. Picture taken, September 2019.

In those few days in Suva, I was fortunate to visit all the places I used to visit as a kid: Thurston Garden, Museum, Wharf, Market, and a few restaurants where I used to love eating. It is true that time goes fast when you are busy and preoccupied. After spending a few days in Suva, it was time to head back to Nadi, and then fly back home. After a four-hour bus ride, we arrived in Nadi. I just had another couple of days with my brother, Nesh.

We wanted to make the most it and try to explore the town of Nadi. We were able to visit, Sri Siva Subramaniya, the largest Hindu temple in Fiji, located in Nadi and attend the kava ceremony at the hotel. Finally, the day arrived for me to fly back. Nesh stayed back, to accompany me to the airport.

We hugged each other, and he said to me with tears in his eyes, "Vinnu, I will miss you terribly. It was so nice to spend the time with you."

We both cried and waved at each other as I walked toward the gate. I saw him standing there, watching until we couldn't see each other anymore.

After getting settled on my flight, I looked outside and said to myself, "Here I go again, leaving the place I love and that was once my home."

Maybe one day, I will be able to alternate living between Florida and Fiji; only time will tell. I fell asleep on the plane, thinking about the great time I had in Fiji, and I was in Los Angeles, California, when I woke up.

In Los Angeles, California, I was able to spend some time with my brothers, Bob and Yogi, and their families. Ten years ago, a few months after my dad passed away, I had made some poor choices and decisions in life, which led to a fall out with Bob's family. As a result, we had not seen each other until now. Since I had a layover in Los Angeles during my trip, I stayed an extra day to visit Bob and his family. Sometimes in life, we are hurting inside, but our pride gets in the way of healing. I had too much pride all those years, not realizing how much time I had lost. In life, sometimes, we are so focused on negative things rather than positive. I am glad that I decided to get out of my comfort zone and visit Bob and his family, as I had a great time, and I felt better afterward. My nephew Neil and I had a great time together, discussing many facts of life. Later on, he appreciated my advice on many things. Despite the fallout, Neil always kept in contact with me. I was glad that we had the opportunity to reconnect after about ten years.

Family is like branches on a tree, we all grow in different directions, yet our roots remain as one.

—ANONYMOUS

After a few days in Los Angeles, I said my goodbyes and headed back to Florida. Following a six-hour flight from Los Angeles, I landed in Fort Lauderdale, Florida. My daughter Mani and one of my colleagues drove two hours from Fort Myers, to pick me up and bring me home. Looking outside through the car windows, I reflected on my trip to Fiji and Los Angeles, and on my brother Nesh, Bob, Yogi, and their families. I missed them, but I was glad to be back home. It is true that there is no place like home. The car finally arrived at my house, which I also call my safe haven. I couldn't ask for anything more in life.

On December 12, 2019, I took a flight from Fort Myers, Florida, to Vancouver. I had not seen my mom and Erin for a while, and Christmas is always a magical time to reconnect with loved ones. I miss both of them dearly. Many things had changed since I saw my mom last. She is in a nursing home, which I had not ever anticipated. I had always seen her cooking and taking care of us, and now she is so dependent on others to take care of her. It is hard to believe what life has ahead of us. My son, Erin, was also going through a difficult time, with his significant other getting diagnosed with stage IV cancer. I prepared myself emotionally and mentally as much as I could. I knew inside that it would be heartbreaking to see my mom in the nursing home, unable to take care of herself. During the flight, all I could think about was my mom. Why does life present us with all this suffering? Why does life seem so unfair? My mom took care of everyone all her life. When it was time for her to enjoy life and do the things she always wanted to do, she was wheelchair-bound. My parents had worked hard all their lives and postponed traveling for later in life, which they were never able to accomplish due to health complications.

One thing I learned from all this is that life is short and unpredictable. Do things while you can. Never leave things for later as that day may never come.

> *Don't die with your music still in you. Don't die with your purpose unfulfilled. Don't die feeling as if your life has been wrong. Don't let that happen to you.*
>
> —Dr. Wayne Dyer

Due to a late flight, I had to spend the night in a hotel. Next morning, eager to see my mom, I took a cab to the nursing home where my mom was. I was unaware that my mom knew that I was coming to visit her. It is impossible to communicate with my mom now, as she does not have a cellular phone. Quickly, I paid the cab driver and walked toward the facility, carrying all my suitcases. The plan was to go to

Veena Sharma

my brother Munna's house later that evening.

As I walked into the room, I saw her sleeping in a room shared with three other elderly females. My mom was lying down in bed. With tears rolling down on my cheeks, I hugged and kissed her. I could see the joy on her face. We both held each other and cried for a while. It was almost breakfast time. My mom and I had breakfast together, and talked about my trip to Fiji, and family. I could sense the disappointment in her voice in not being able to do things as she used to.

Visiting my mom in Vancouver, Canada, December 2019.

The next day, I met Erin for coffee. Though he was hiding his feeling, I could see the sadness in his eyes, knowing that his significant other was slipping away slowly. We sat and talked for a long time. I reassured him that I was there for him anytime he needed me. I must say that no matter how old children get, for parents, they are still little kids. Once a parent, always a parent. I missed my daughter Moni terribly while visiting my mom and Erin in Vancouver. It seemed like yesterday when we were all together. Moni lives in Henrico, Virginia now. She works as a registered nurse and is in family nurse practitioner program. I am planning to visit her after I return back home. After few days of spending quality time with my mom, Erin, and rest of the family, I headed back to Fort Myers, Florida, my home now. I consider it my safe haven. Again, I am thankful to everyone who has crossed my path. Without them, I would have never found myself.

GOLDEN NUGGET

Don't let obstacles and challenges in your life demotivate you. Instead, look at it as an opportunity to grow. You will harvest what you plant. Life is all about what you make of it. Learn to believe in yourself and trust your feelings. Spend time with friends and family while you can. Nothing is more precious than the moments spent with loved ones.

CONCLUSION

Follow Your Dreams

Your life is like a play with several acts. Some of the characters who enter have short roles to play, others, much larger. Some are villains and others are good guys. But all of them are necessary; otherwise, they wouldn't be in the play. Embrace them all, and move on to the next act.

—DR. WAYNE DYER

Writing this book has not been easy. It has brought back many memories of the past. It took me back to many positive and negative times but once again reaffirmed the things I did in life and the reasons for which I did them. It almost seemed like putting a puzzle together; there was a purpose for everything that happened in my life. I was sailing through the storm, and now have finally reached my destination, despite all the turbulence. My whole life had been about trying to find myself, through ups and downs, and trials and errors. Unlike in the past, I have created a perfect balance in life now. I am happier, content, calm, grounded, ego-free. I have adapted a positive mindset and avoid all kinds of negative influences. In other words, I have found my purpose in life.

Happiness is not something you get in life; happiness is something you bring in life.

—Dr. Wayne Dyer

My plan in the future is to continue to follow my dreams by doing what I love to do. My goal is to travel to places I have never been, enjoy the beauty around me, continue to strengthen my relationship with my loved ones, and help people who are in need. One of my biggest future goals is to go on a retreat trip, where I will stay in a place on a mountain, surrounded by pure, natural beauty, where I can do yoga, eat healthy, exercise, practice meditation, and work on my next book. I am a firm believer that you have to take care of yourself first, before you can take care of someone else.

Honor the physical temple that houses you by eating healthfully, exercising, listening to your body's needs, and treating it with dignity and love.

—Dr. Wayne Dyer

I hope to inspire, empower, and motivate people to make the best of their lives. To live life to the fullest without any regrets.

Moving forward, I am planning to live my life by these life affirmations:

I will always take care of myself

I will always offer help to the ones in need

I will always believe in myself

I will always surround myself with positivity

I will always nourish my mind, body, and soul

I will give myself space to grow and learn

I will never harm anyone

I will lead a respectful and honest life

I will allow myself to be who I am

I have the power to create change

I will always respect others

I am at peace with who I am

I am grateful to have my family and friends.

I will live my passion

GOLDEN NUGGET

Live your life to the fullest. Enjoy little things in life. Don't dwell in the past. Keep moving forward in life. Separate positivity from negativity. Embrace every experience in life, either positive or negative. Think of as a unique experience; learn and grow from that.

She believed she could and so she did

She broke free from the chains

She shirked the thoughts that went before

She took life by the reigns

She challenged every obstacle

She broke down every wall

She shook the cries of 'you can't do it'

She didn't fear the fall

She failed to fail, she proved them wrong

She bared her heart to all

She showed the world she'd had enough

If she couldn't run, she'd crawl

She lit the night with passion bright

She sometimes cried and cowered

But never, did she give up hope

She blossomed and she flowered

—DONNA ASHWORTH

Made in the USA
Columbia, SC
27 June 2020

10934135R00085